9.1.1. COMPLETE GUIDE
to NATURAL HEALING

VIE LORIOT DE ROUVRAY

9.1.1. Complete Guide to Natural Healing
Copyright © 2022 by VIE Loriot de Rouvray

All rights reserved. No part of this publication may be reproduced, distributed, or transmitted in any form or by any means, including photocopying, recording, or other electronic or mechanical methods, without the prior written permission of the author, except in the case of brief quotations embodied in critical reviews and certain other non-commercial uses permitted by copyright law.

ISBN
978-1-956161-82-3 (Paperback)
978-1-956161-81-6 (eBook)

www.instituteoflightandsound.com

The purpose of this guide is to educate and inform you. It is about preparing you for the shift of energy and beyond the ascension.

How can we explain to the unprepared person the meeting—reunion of two angels—with one common mission?

Two gifted souls, blessed with special gifts from *God,* came together for the purpose of *light and the sound frequency healing.* To remove all energetic blockages in your body and to accrete the amount of light, activate your DNA from two to twelve at least, to raise your vibrations before the reconnection and to access the fifth dimension. This therapy adjusts the body's oscillation by sound and music and color light harmonics frequency with sacred geometric forms and energy. Sound and light resonant vibration change the human brain and body. Harmonic frequencies rapidly rebalance and restore the natural energies of your body and mind. Sound waves amplify the effects upon acupressure points and relax muscles, increase circulation, and reduce inflammation.

I am VIE, the first Aquarius to come with something that humanity will take over two thousand years to process. I am a metaphysical, intuitive light and vibration healer. I am gifted in the new vibratory transformation frequency that I work on, with the cosmic doctors and Nikola Tesla.

I was asked to write this holistic and spiritual guide by my spiritual family at the end of my eighteen months and daily initiation by Archangel Michael for CHADD and me.

Nearly three years later, I am putting this guide together with the help of my coworker, CHADD, after two cancers in my family, several Alzheimer's and Parkinson's disease cases among my relatives, and because of what happened to CHADD.

CHADD has been kept on psychiatric drugs since he was five years old, placed in many different locations and various facilities, kept in a foggy state, and finally court-ordered to take his medications. Thirty-two years later, he tried to stop all drugs and reached for help through the state and county. At eighteen years old, due to drugs that were keeping him in a depressive state, he tried to kill himself and went into a coma.

CHADD is an intuitive healer and, when he came out of the coma and back to life, was gifted in the area of sound frequency—as a healing tool for humanity bringing back powerful messages from God to humanity. He is an energy retracting transducer of God.

We have been both Baker Acted and intoxicated in a very well-known hotel in Florida and sent to jail twice. (You will understand better and why this has happened to us when you read that it happened also to Dr. Loïc le Ribault—when he tried to have his research known and his product G5 available to the public, though he was working with the FBI and it began healing so many people where traditional medicine would not work.)

I was wearing that day, and as usual, my powerful energetic tools from Tibet around my neck. This Tibetan tools was enhancing my own energy to such a point that it has been removed and taken away from me by the police and never returned. This tool was attracting the eyes of everyone and was awakening people at the same time.

I must say that during the last seven years, I have been part of many conventions in various locations and different states with my Tibetan tools in public and presenting and working the light and the sound using sacred geometric forms, connecting people to their angels, cleansing blood and DNA, and reconnecting the two parts of the brain. Our holistic health and energy work must have been considered a treat to the drug companies and to other authorities in power or key places. They fear our knowledge and our power, as we work on many levels, including on a metaphysical plane, and because the sound and the light triggers a new sense of awareness to another layer of reality.

CHADD had been asked to remove his ankh, and it was never returned. I had been asked by some religious people to stop my energy work and even told that it was a gift of the dark!

We are both reconnected to the Divine, and we are here on a humanitarian mission. We are the chosen ones. We have an energy exchange at the heart center. We are here to help you all for the ascension, the shift of energy, and beyond.

You have been kept in lies and in the dark. We are here to help you and to tell you the truth.

OUR CAREER FOCUS

Our Humanitarian Mission

It is spiritual and somewhat holistic in the process.

To inform, educate, and introduce you to what is available to today:

- Divine reconnection (to your angels, activate your pineal gland, and activate your DNA)
- Sound frequencies
- Music, light, and biosound therapy
- Chromotherapy
- Phosphenes
- Essential oils
- Bach flower essences

The future of healing lies in yourself. Light and sound are energy and frequencies. They are cells communication and speak to the cells in the body.

Pray to Saint Michael for Protection (every day)

Saint Michael the Archangel, defend me in battle
Be my protection against the wickedness and snares of the devil
May God rebuke him I humbly pray
And do thou Saint Michael, prince of the heavenly host
By the power of God cast into hell Satan and all the other evil spirits and entities
Who prowl throughout the world seeking the ruin of souls.
Amen.

3D (Dimension) = Fear   5D = Love and Peace

The frequency of the sound is a very powerful tool. Notes are colors and frequency. Like light is also sound. Our body is mostly energy.

Most of Nikola Tesla's technology has been used by the military in the US for space and military in highly confidential aspects and has never been released to the public! Nikola Tesla came forth a century and a half ago and was the first born to bring many technologies to the planet for humanity to establish "liberation." Many of his ideas, the technology, came as he was able to tap into consciousness, which held of this knowledge. He saw himself as a transformer that transforms it to a state. This is the gift that was given to him. And know he came to see that some of these had a military perspective that began to concern him.

HAARP (High Frequency Active Auroral Research Project) and North Polar Ozone Depletion, Weather Disruption, and Electromagnetic Warfare By Adam Trombly and Project Earth Network Scientists

"HAARP is also a weapon of mass destruction. Radio waves strong enough to cause earthquakes are controlled by the US military. It's the largest ionospheric heater in the world. What they have found is that by sending radio frequency energy up and focusing it, as they do with these kinds of instruments, it causes a heating effect. And that heating literally lifts the ionosphere within a 30-mile diameter area therein changing localized pressure systems or perhaps the route of jet streams. The problem is we cannot model the system adequately. Long term consequences of atmospheric heating are unknown. And HAARP has already been accused of modifying the weather."

Bruce Tainio has determined that the average frequency of the human body during the day time is 62–68 Hz (a healthy body frequency is 62–72 Hz). When the frequency drops, the immune system is compromised. If the frequency drops to 58 Hz, cold and flu symptoms appear. At 55 Hz, diseases like candida take hold, at 52 Hz, Epstein-Barr, and at 42 Hz, cancer. According to Dr. Royal Rife, every disease has a frequency. He found that certain frequencies can prevent the development of disease and that others would destroy disease.

Since atomic radiation, that we have created with atomic bomb, etc., we are losing our immune system. Grey alien exist, and they are not dangerous to us; they are simply making some test and have implanted around 250 people on the planet just for test, but they are not dangerous to human beings implanted. They are very interested on what we do to remedy because they are dying by lack of immune system, like many human beings, due to the atomic radiation that we have created. The planet destroys itself with atomic destruction.

It is important to recognize you are creating your own reality. You create everything in your life. This can be difficult for many people to grasp when they first come across it, but there is no accident.

A new earth is being created, and we are moving into another dimension. Vibration and frequency of the earth is changing; time is faster.

DNA is changing and we also have to change. Most people are caught in a wheel of *karma* (stuck with emotions from the past). They have been here and lived on earth for hundreds and hundreds of years, and they do not work on it, though getting rid of it is forgiveness and letting go. It serves no purpose anymore.

Isis is called the Mother of All Healing. She was in Egypt and in Atlantis at the time Mary Magdalene was on earth. During her time in Atlantis, she was acting as a teacher and had connection to Sirius. Mary Magdalene was also a teacher and she was married to Jesus, and they were forged by those who wished to shut down their public working energy. Part of their mission was to change the DNA of human being. History repeats itself.

The DNA Quantum Field (The Merkaba)

Activated DNA is not just biology, not just a molecule, but the carrier of all that is spiritual in every single human being.

Your Akashic record is there. Everything you've ever done is there. All your life lessons are there. Your spiritual core is there. Your angelic name is there; extraterrestrial (ET) energy is there.

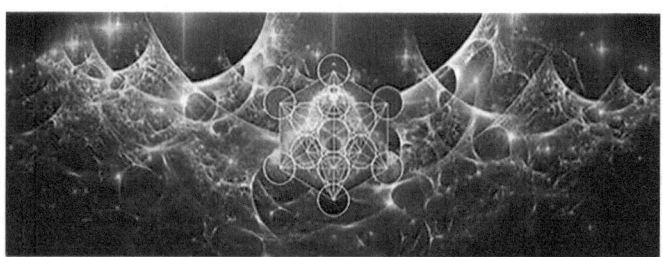

TRUTH AND FACTS

Our children are poisoned at birth with vaccination shots, which contain mercury and much more, and many are autistic then after. An article by Dr. Joseph Mercola, "Culprits of Autism Identified: Toxins, Gut Bacteria, Nutritional Deficiencies, and Vaccines Made with Human Fetal Cell Lines" on October 6, 2014, discusses this. Children's bodies cannot reject the mercury injected in their system.

Mercury is the most toxic element second only after plutonium. Then there are all of the other toxic components in all vaccines, including aluminum, which is constantly shown in studies to exist in high levels in autism and Alzheimer's, along with mercury. And then there is the squalene in the swine flu vaccines.

Vitamin D is linked to mortality. Vitamin D deficiency can be associated with a significant risk of cardiovascular disease and reduced survival. Dr. Erin D. Michos, MD, for John Hopkins Medicine, says that recent evidence supports an association between vitamin D deficiency and hypertension, peripheral vascular disease, diabetes mellitus, metabolic syndrome, coronary artery disease, and heart failure.

Dr. Blaylock, a board-certified neurosurgeon, says that nobody should take a vaccine for swine flu. It has one of the most dangerous vaccine immune components called MF-59, which proved to be a component that causes autoimmune diseases like MS (multiple sclerosis), rheumatic arthritis, and lupus. It is vaccine that has been thought to be highly associated with the Gulf War syndrome, which killed more than ten thousand soldiers and caused a 200 percent increase in serious diseases. This is the H1N1 virus that causes Chinese syndrome.

Scientific teams of Calgary have demonstrated that concentration of low mercury is able to destroy brain cells. The mercury, in low dosage, is able to damage the nervous system connections and create cerebral damage and is the origin, in particular, of the neurodegenerative illness like Alzheimer's or Parkinson's disease. The mercury density in a vaccine is 25 percent higher than the level required to be considered hazardous waste. This is directly injected into the bloodstream of infants, children, expectant mothers, and senior citizen.

The main purpose of the vaccination, in general, is to trigger an immune system response, and there are many side effects that can develop, local and general reactions.

Local reaction ranges from pain at the injection site to inflammation, redness, swelling, abscess formation, or alteration.

Vaccine reactions that affect all the body may include nausea, fever, development of adjuvant-related arthritis, allergic reactions, organ-specific toxicity, anaphylaxis, immune suppression, and introduction of autoimmune diseases.

We are left, today, with few antibiotics, and soon with the energy shift of the planet, traditional medicine/drugs will not work anymore. We hope that this guide will help you prepare and keep you in perfect health.

Let us look to the social context in which we live with these wonderful substances. People on their spiritual way quickly learn that what we leave out of our brains, our bodies, and our spirits is as important as what we put inside it. In reality, the war against drugs is not really a war against drugs. It is a very small part of them among thousands of medications approved by the FDA. The prescription drugs remain drugs, and many of them have important side effects, which are supposed to cure. One medication, one drug, is artificially a chemical drug and a big profit for the manufacturer.

Herbs on the other hand are natural plants that still have natural properties untouched. Prescribed drugs damage more than they cure and require other prescriptions to counteract the side effects and so on. It is a vicious cycle. In the name of legal drugs, far more people die from prescribed drugs than from legal drugs, "the herbs."

Many Illnesses Unexplained Today Can Be Related to Ingestion of Drugs

The medicine by frequency of sound and color light, when applied correctly to the right meridian, has no side effects because they do not address the symptoms but get to the cause directly, where the energy has been cut. In offering the element in the body through the light, the body choose what he needs and the quantity that he needs.

The therapy by frequency and energy of the light and the sound as natural medicine restore and balance the energy that the body needs without harmfulness of chemical products and of the drugs because it is gently given and not forced in the digestive tract, the blood, and the tissues. As homeopathy or acupuncture, the therapy by frequency of the light and the sound is based on a concept of chemical imbalance, a state of illness and energy of vibration none appropriate in the body. The illness starts when the energy of the body absorbs the light and reacts to the frequency of the sound. When the energy is absorbed, its level is raised before soon returning in its normal sate.

All illnesses at their initial state are attributed to the imbalance of the etheric fields or to the health of the aura at the energy level.

At the contrary, the allopathic medicine use treatments only to the physical level, like the surgery and the medications, that very often cleans without curing. To understand why surgery and prescriptions drugs often slow down, or even unable the person to heal, here is an example: to successfully rebalance the energy (the cause of illnesses), the technique of the forty-ninth vibration begins at the highest vibratory levels (etheric).

LIFESAVING INFORMATION ABOUT NONPATENTABLE NATURAL THERAPIES HAS BEEN WITHHELD

....

The human body does not produce its own vitamin C (ascorbic acid), and because of this lack of knowledge, almost all humans suffer from vitamin C deficiency and are susceptible of cardiovascular and other diseases.

The human body does not produce natural amino acids, such as lysine, and almost all humans suffer from lysine deficiency and are susceptible to cancer and other diseases.

Nonpatentable natural therapies have been discredited with the goal to protect and expand business with disease based on patented drugs.

Coronary Heart Disease

The primary cause of coronary artery disease and heart attacks is structural weakening of the impaired function wall, which—similar to scurvy—develops as the result of long-term deficiencies of vitamins and other nutrients. The worldwide death toll from cardiovascular is in excess of twelve million lives every year.

High Blood Pressure

The primary cause of high blood pressure is an increased tension of the artery wall due to a deficiency of essential nutrients in the artery smooth muscle cells, leading to narrowing wall of the artery diameter and a rise in blood pressure. A multitude of clinical studies are available documenting the benefits of nonpatentable micronutrients, in particular the amino acid arginine and magnesium. They correct the underlying deficiency in millions of vascular wall cells, thereby relaxing the blood vessel walls, increasing blood vessel diameter, and helping to normalize high blood pressure. The pharmaceutical drugs focus on treatment of symptoms, and beta-blockers reduce the heart rate and diuretics reduce the blood volume. These pharmaceutical drugs avoid correcting the "spasms" of the blood vessel walls, which is the primary cause of high blood pressure. And the drugs have long terms detrimental side effects causing a multitude of new diseases.

Heart Failure

Lack of cellular biocatalysts, certain vitamins, minerals, carnitine, coenzyme Q10, and other bioenergy carriers in millions of heart muscles cells results in impaired heart pumping function and accumulation of water in the body.

Diuretics marketed for the treatment of heart failure not only eliminate the water in the body but also flush out vitamins, minerals, and other water-soluble bioenergy carriers.

Irregular Heartbeat

Lack of micronutrients, vitamins, minerals, ubiquinone, and other bioenergy will carry in millions of electrical heart muscle cells. It results in impaired generation or conduction of the electrical impulses required for normal heartbeat. Dr. Thomas Moore, in his book *Deadly Medicine*, explains why worldwide, over one hundred million patients with regular heartbeat remain uncured.

Cancer

It is a scientific fact that all cancers spread by the same mechanism, the use of collagen-digesting enzymes (collagenase, metalloproteinase). The therapeutic use of the natural amino acid *lysine* can block these enzymes and thereby inhibit the spread of the cancer cells. The only reason why this breakthrough in medicine has not been investigated further and applied in the treatment of cancer patients worldwide is the fact that these substances are not patentable.

AIDS and Other Infections Diseases

Vitamin C is able to reduce the replication of the HIV virus by more than 99 percent. This fact has been known for more than a decade. And to enhance immunity against infectious diseases is an optimum intake of vitamins B6, B12, folic acid, and certain other essential nutrients. These biocatalysts of cellular metabolism increase the production of leucocytes.

Diabetes

Diabetes is a blood sugar imbalance. Super B vitamin supports pancreas function, and goji berry tea helps prevent diabetes. Diabetes is not common in China, where wolfberry is consumed regularly. Organic silica Silicium G5 liquid has very good results.

Nerve Pain:

Try CoQ10 400 mg taken in one serving the first day up to a few months, then reduce the dosage to 200 mg to keep the positive effect. Also take organic Silicium G5.

Cholesterol

Red rice extract works very well.

Charcoal Is the Incredible Healer:
Charcoal Is the Most Powerful Poison Pump

Using an activated form of this natural product, doctors are treating everything from gas and intestinal ailments to serious infections.

The French chemist Claude Bertrand swallows one teaspoonful of arsenic, enough to kill 150 men. He was not committing suicide but was conducting an experiment. He lived to tell us. He survived because the arsenic was mixed with charcoal. The charcoal acted as a sponge in his stomach and sucked up the arsenic before it reached his blood.

Parkinson's Disease (PD)

Parkinson's disease is a progressive neurodegenerative disorder characterized by progressive selective loss of dopaminergic neurons in the substantia nigra, and some clinical trials are currently ongoing in Parisian hospitals using *bee venom in the treatment of Parkinson's disease.*

Safe Breast Cancer Screening

This is possible through the new automated breast ultrasound for cancer screening. It is harmless, painless, and safe for everyone. Many physicians have bought into the myth that mammography prevents breast cancer, but by the time a lesion is even detectable by mammography, we are looking at average rate of growth between eight to nine years. To prevent the disease, the suggestion is to take adequate amounts of daily vitamin D, drinking five to six cups of green tea a day, and eating two tablespoons of organic ground flaxseeds. It's the over x-raying and xenoestrogens in our food and air that contribute to the high incidence.

The way to Keep your Immune System High, and Keep you Healthy

Combination of supplements to take everyday:

Vit. C
Vit. D3
Zinc
Quercitin
Magnesium
Atomidine (Iodine)

Use Essential oil Thieves (inhale, or put 1-2 drops on your wrists) Sanitize your hands with the Thieves wipe.

A Good Protocol to use after a Vaccination Shot

Apply immediately around the injection some Essential oil of Purification and Thieves. Put some clay in a bowl of water soak a clean small piece of cloth in 30 minutes. Apply to the arm and band it. When it's dry discard everything. (Never use it twice) Adult take 2 activated charcoal in capsule.

Use daily some antiviral Essential oils like Ravintsara, Tea tree or the blend called Thieve

THE PERSECUTION AND RESISTANCE OF LORC LE RIBAULT BY MARTIN J. WALKER

In 1985 while working as an independent forensic scientist for the French judiciary, Loïc le Ribault joined forces with a highly acclaimed research chemist, Professor Norbert Duffaut from the University of Bordeaux. Between them, they hoped to develop their common work on organic silica, a substance which they believed had a wide range of therapeutic uses.

After twelve years of work together, perhaps as a consequence of their work on the new therapy, Duffaut was *dead, poisoned* in suspicious circumstances and Le Ribault himself had suffered two months solitary confinement in a French j*ail*.

> I shall continue my actions of distributing OS5 despite all the opposition. I do it for all those patients for whom I have the opportunity and honor of caring, those who were abandoned by modern medicine which was unable to offer them a cure or who found the orthodox treatments offered worse than the illness itself.

Loïc le Ribault, France's most renowned forensic scientist and specialist in the study of silica, holds court in the dingy surroundings of the Flying Fish pub on the harbor in Saint Helier, Jersey. With a Gaelic shrug and in faltering English, he explains how the pub has become his home and his office.

He knows almost everyone in the bar, he knows the bus drivers, the local shopkeepers and many of the harbor's boat owners. He knows them, he says, "*because I have treated them, for this illness and that illness. Many of them I have cured with OS5.*"

Silicium Laboratories LLC's Organic Silica fifth generation molecule was invented by the late Dr. Loïc Le Ribault.

Throughout the nineteen eighties, Loïc Le Ribault was the most important and renowned forensic scientist in France. He collaborated with the FBI and was greatly admired by his American colleagues. This collaboration and admiration was expressed by the Pulitzer winner, John McPhee, in his book *Irons in the Fire,* 1998. As a precocious young academic with a love for silica, Le Ribault had ground-breaking papers published by the French Academy of Science. At twenty-four, in 1971, he discovered a new function for the electron scanning microscope (ESM), called exoscopy, which enabled him to discern the history of grains of sand.

The following year, in 1972, while working with sand on the ESM, Le Ribault made an interesting discovery: a layer of water-soluble amorphous silica which contained micro-organisms covered the surface of some sand grains. He found that these microorganisms and the secretions which they left on the sand contained organic silica. Organic silica differs from mineral silica which makes up the majority of the earth's crust, in that it contains carbon and can be readily assimilated by animals.

By 1975, Le Ribault had created a process by which it was possible to recover these deposits from the surface of the sand. All of this work was accepted by the scientific establishment and his papers published by the French Academy of Science.

There has been constant research into organic silica over the previous fifty years and some of this research had raised questions about its therapeutic use. In his early work, as a geologist, Le Ribault had not been following the research into silica and health. However, in the early eighties, while working on the organic silica deposits he had found, he immersed his hands in an organic silica solution and found that his psoriasis was cured. From then on, le Ribault's work became focused in the therapeutic properties of silica.

AGAINST AGING MECHANISMS

Silicium G5: Antiaging Properties

Silicium G5 Living Silica is a fundamental part of the antiaging program created by nutritional expert Victoria Baras, author of the European best seller *Antiaging Natural*.

Fifth generation of organic silica is well-known in fighting sclerosis of the tissues. This destructuring action is caused by two important mechanisms: lipidic peroxidation and nonenzymatic glycosylation. The glycosylation phenomenon begins in the thirties and increases with age. It reduces the elasticity of the arteries and the skin. Silicium G5 slows down the glycosylation phenomenon.

Silica is an excellent antidote of aluminum and other heavy metals that accumulate in our tissues. Silica *cleans* the heavy metals and eliminates them. This has been demonstrated in diverse studies. In the magazine *Nutrition Today,* Forrest Nielsen considers it as a good prevention against Alzheimer's disease and other senile degenerations.

This molecule, now known as fifth-generation organic silica, is the best known product in Europe and the most efficient way to take silica. It has a 70 percent assimilation rate compared to the 5–20 percent rate found with other silica molecules on the market.

Le Ribault repeatedly tested and refined his organic silica molecule until he had the safest and highest bioavailable form on the market. He gave lectures and taught courses throughout the world. He authored eleven books and published dozens of well-received scientific studies. The last conference he held was in Barcelona on May 20, 2005, in the exhibition hall to five hundred doctors and professional nutritionists. He died in 2007.

Silicium G5 Liquid 1000 ml

Silica is an essential ingredient in our body structure and metabolism (also present in animals and plants). It is a basic component of every cell in the body and helps assimilate other essential minerals such as magnesium, phosphorus, and calcium.

Thus, it strengthens the bones, maintains elastin and collagen in cartilage and muscles, and ensures healthy tissue in skin, hair, arteries, internal organs and endocrine glands, and in the brain and nervous system.

However, as the body ages, it loses its silica content, which contributes to the onset in later years of stiff and painful joints, dry skin and hair, brittle bones, heart problems, and increased susceptibility to infection, disease, fatigue, stroke, loss of memory and cognitive function, and so on.

To replenish its supply of silica, the body needs to absorb it in its organic form, which is not available in adequate amounts in our usual diet. This is why the G5 formula of organic silica, developed by the French scientist Dr. Loïc Le Ribault, is so useful in maintaining all round health and counteracting many types of disease and symptoms of aging. For more than fifteen years, Dr. Le Ribault's organic silica products have been used, internally and externally, by tens of thousands of people all over the world, often with astonishing results.

This product is the fifth generation of G5, providing organic silica in a form easier to absorb and more effective than that found in colloidal silica, silical acid, or high-silica plant extracts, and with none of their side effects. G5 organic silica products have *no* side effects, even after being used for many years, and are compatible with any other treatment that may be prescribed.

Ingredients: pure water, organic silica.

The more than thirty years of science behind our Silicium line of organic silica products comes from cutting-edge research conducted at numerous prestigious institutions and the application of this research by world-renowned scientist Loïc Le Ribault. The results are exceptional, organic products manufactured to the highest standards for safety, optimal bioavailability, and effectiveness.

Specific disorders can be augmented or caused by inadequate nutrition and Silicium Laboratories have always taken a holistic approach to helping with complementary therapies. As a best in class nutritional supplement provider, Silicium Laboratories is committed to offering the most effective organic silica products in the world. They are proud to contribute to the creation of healthier lives within the global community. Silicium Laboratories is guided by the vision of enhancing the physical, psychological, social, and spiritual well-being of people everywhere through natural health care.

Thanks to Loïc Le Ribault, fifth generation organic silica is now available in the USA, UK, and worldwide.

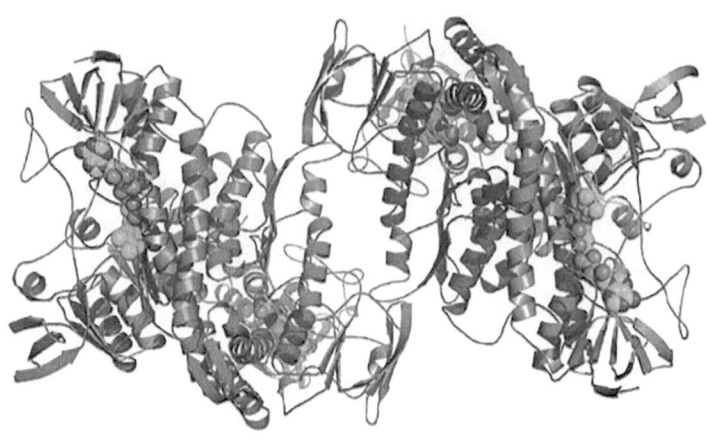

WHAT CAN ENZYMES DO?

1. Clean clogged arteries of plaque
2. Empty stomach of undigested fat
3. Prevent stroke and heart attack
4. Enzymes eliminate old fat and proteins left deposited from years, causing cardiovascular problems (Taussig and Nepier, 1979).
5. Protease reduces inflammation processes and enhances circulation and the immune system by improving and increasing the surface area of the red blood cell, allowing it to transport more oxygen (Sulfreurdd and Taussig-Morris, 1978).
6. Enzymes are effective in weight regulation; overweight people are lacking in lipase.
7. Enzymes prevent allergies and degeneration.

Cleansing the Colon and Liver

1. Enzymes help clear the body of undigested proteins and meats.
2. Undigested starches, sugars, and carbohydrates will ferment fats, turning them rancid.
3. Toxins create a host for disease such as candida, leaky gut, brain fog, fatigue, hypoglycemia, depression, allergies, and fibromyalgia.

KEEP YOUR KIDNEYS KICKING BY GLENYS BROWN

Top tips discussed why and how the kidneys need to be kept warm, with particular care in winter. Cold, windy, wet, extreme conditions all can have a negative effect on the efficiency of the kidneys. Unfortunately, it may be some time, even years, before you realize the kidneys have been weakened.

The kidneys and adrenals react to what is stressful for you. Some stress is normal and the kidneys will cope and stay in balance. Modern living now makes it difficult for the energy balance to be maintained. For example, when you intake caffeine, it sets up a danger alert from the kidney adrenals to the brain that more adrenaline is needed to be produced. This brings an adrenaline rush and depletes the kidney-adrenal healthy balance.

1. *Massage Your Kidneys*

Place both palms of hands together and rub them briskly until they are very hot. Place hot palms on to the middle of your back at the waistline. Rub your palms up and down the middle of your back for 36 times. Begin with 10 times and gradually build up. This tip is great to do what at the computer. It only takes seconds and your back benefits more each time you do it.

2. *Massage Your Feet*

Why massage my feet when my kidneys are in my back, you may ask. The start of your kidney channel, which brings energy into the kidneys, is on the soles of your feet. Look at the sole of one foot and squeeze your toes. Then look at the pad of the top of the foot and there will be a small indent in the middle of the foot at the base of the pad (about one third down your foot). This is the Kidney 1 point that connects with Earth energy and supplies energy to your kidneys to build them up and reduce stress. Bubbling spring is one of the names given this in Chinese medicine, a name that describes it perfectly as it is where energy is gathered and bubbles up into your body. If you think about walking and jumping the Bubbling Spring point is where your feet "spring" from as they move.

To Massage: Use the palm of your hand on the bottom of the heel of the opposite foot. Rub palm firmly from the heel up until off the toes. Repeat up to 100 times. Start with what feels right to you and build up gradually each day. This massage also does wonders for your circulation. When done before retiring to sleep it encourages calm sound sleep.

3. *Turn Your Energy Over*

This is a great practice as you can do it almost any time you want to as no one can observe it happening, yet it can have a profound effect on reducing stress thus benefits the kidneys and adrenals.

To turn your energy over notice when you have a thought or hear a sound, or get a feeling which, for you, is negative.

Immediately think or say "Thanks for the message" as this is your body's way of letting you know something needs attention. Then think of a phrase you believe is positive about yourself. Begin with the physical body (e.g., I love it when my eyes twinkle. Or I like my hair. Or I like the way I walk.) Repeat your positive phrase three times. This works as it lifts your energy and stops the negative phrase being internalized and adding to a deeper, stressful pattern. Use any of these tips when you feel your energy needs a boost. Commit to doing one of them daily. Gradually you will find you not only feel better, these practices have taken such a little effort and time to keep your stress down and your eyes smiling.

CANCER AND THE IMPORTANCE OF EMOTIONS (TRAUMAS, ANXIETY, STRESS, DEPRESSION)

Human beings have become increasingly dependent upon people and drugs outside of us, instead of the miraculous, Creator-given self-healing mechanisms within us.

The real cause of cancer and other diseases is an "unexpected traumatic shock for which humans are emotionally unprepared." In the vast majority of cancer patients, there is a combination of both psychological and physiological stresses that have contributed, at the cellular level, to depletion of adrenaline, excess sugar, and lack of oxygen—causing individual cells to mutate and become cancerous.

Factors that contribute to a normal cell becoming depleted of adrenaline, high in sugar, and low in oxygen include poor nutrition, toxins, EMF radiation, lack of exercise, and lack of sunlight. Psychological stressors include (but are not limited to) inescapable shock (loss of loved one, divorce), repressed feelings, depression, poor sleep, emotional trauma, etc. This "inescapable shock" happens two years before the cancer diagnosis. Some say up to twenty years. This sets up a vicious cycle.

The cycle begins with the inescapable shock / emotional trauma that affects deep sleep and the production of melatonin within the body. Again, melatonin is necessary for inhibiting cancer cell growth and is the primary hormone responsible for regulating the immune system. During phase 1, the emotional reflex center in the brain slowly breaks down, creating a dark "spot" on the brain. This theory has been proven with every cancer patient because these dark spots were visible on X-rays and brain scans. Each part of the emotional reflex center in the brain controls and is connected to an organ or part of the body, and when the emotion center breaks down, so does communication to the organ or body part it is connected to. The immune system also receives subconscious messages from the emotion center to slow down or even stop working.

Remember, when the human body is faced with the stress of an inescapable shock, the hormone cortisol helps to decide two options—fight or flight—and shuts down any functions that might get in the way. If you feel (on a subconscious level) like you have somehow "died" emotionally, your brain sends messages to shut down your immune system. When you shut down your immune system, viruses, bacteria, and yeast take over.

The best way is to live as our ancestors did as much as possible. Get out in the sun first thing in the morning. Go outside and take a break when the sun comes up. Eat during the day when possible. Eat natural and organic and avoid white sugar and all artificial sweeteners. Soak all your fruit and vegetable in baking soda (no aluminum), and rinse them well before eating, or cook them.

Licensed Mental Health Counseling, Psychologists

Psychologists, licensed professional counselors, licensed clinical professional counselors, or licensed mental health counselors provide mental health with substance abuse care (psychotropic drugs that are poison to the DNA) to millions of Americans. Licensed professional counselors (LPCs) are doctoral and master's level mental health service providers, trained to work with individuals and behaviors. LPCs make up a large percentage of the workforce employed in community mental health centers, agencies, and organizations.

Deborah Kory said, "I first wrote about psychologists and torture for the *Huffington Post* back in 2007 when I was working toward my doctorate in clinical psychology and all hell was breaking loose around revelations that psychologists were involved in torture at Guantanamo Bay and other CIA black sites. I had just started writing my dissertation, which sought to explore the history and social forces that led to such insanity in the profession I was immersing so much time, money and energy into making my vocation.

"I frankly had hoped the whole issue would be resolved by now—the perpetrators would be in prison, the system would be reformed so that it could never happen again, psychologists would have organized and taken a powerful stand against this misuse of power in their name. Yet here we are, 10 years after the first revelations of torture appeared in the media, my dissertation long since bound in obscurity in my school's library, and not only are the revelations still coming, there is only now the first hint of a real investigation into the specific role psychologists played in this process. With the release of the Torture Report, also known as the Senate's highly-redacted executive summary from the 'Committee Study of the Central Intelligence Agency's Detention and Interrogation Program,' I realized it would be morally remiss of me not to take this brief minute when the public eye is trained on this issue to share some information with you.

"Psychologists, psychotherapists, anyone professing to have an interest in the psyche, which is the Greek word for soul, simply have no business being anywhere near torture, either in spirit or law. Given that things have only gotten worse politically and economically over the last decade, with violent extremism at an all-time high, there is nothing to keep this from happening again."

MINERALS, OXYGEN, AND BLOOD FLOW WILL GIVE YOU HEALTH AND PROSPERITY

Minerals, Oxygen, and Blood Flow

Without proper *minerals,* the red blood cells stick together and it causes a heaviness, rendering the oxygenating of the cells pretty much futile.

Breathing deeply does more than just oxygenate your blood. And you should breathe deeply to *oxygenate* your blood. Every few minutes, take an oxygen break. By doing that, deep breathing signals relaxation and will go to your entire nervous system. When you feel relaxed, it is easier to move into higher states of joy and gratitude. When you are in the state of joy and gratitude, you attract all good things to you!

Get some absorbable minerals into your body and breathe. Make sure the minerals are from a food source and not chemically created. Like pure *spirulina* is a very good absorbable source and the cost is minimal. Spirulina is from the sea, contains a full array of minerals, and yet has very low sodium.

Breathing

Sit up straight, or lie down flat. Breathe deeply in and out several times, three or more when it comes to breathing exercises.

Breathe in and hold, then forcefully expel all the air from your lungs by pulling in your abdominal muscles. This gets the old stale air out and makes way for clean air.

Elements have consciousness. Bless the air, just like you do your food and drink, and ask for the most beneficial parts to be brought into your body.

Our wonderful tool, our jewelry pendant will diffuse the perfect amount of scent of pure essential oils to protect you in all public places—waiting rooms, hospitals, in travel, conventions—against bacteria, viruses, etc., and will clean the air that you breath. (Our limited edition Ascension 911 essential oil jewelry is enhanced by a diamond. The stone will keep you crystal clear on Christ.)

A Miraculous Method to Learn

Touch fingers of your right hand to just below the left cheek bone. At same time, put fingers of right hand just under the same side collarbone. Hold for one to twenty minutes, whatever is comfortable.

Then reverse and touch fingers of your left hand to just below the right cheek bone and your right hand fingers to just below the right collarbone.

No pressure, just contact, completing a circuit. Sometimes you can feel the pulses when both are the same, you have it. Open circuit, no longer stuck.

Use it for the following:

- Sinus congestion
- Coughing
- Diabetes (also just hold your thumb, weird, but it works)
- Excessive talking
- Stomach problems
- Allergies
- Lips (dry, cracked lips are a sign of stomach/sinus flow need)
- Bipolar disorders
- And many other things

The Benefit of This Method

Reduction of the appetite and brings less calories; pure proteins are effective against water retention and cellulite (It is also why women like it a lot).

With this method, you must drink at least one gallon of water per day. The proteins and the water together helps to eliminate the cellulite and to the urination elimination. Also, the proteins help to the penetration of the water into tissue.

WHAT IS HO'OPONOPONO?

Ho'oponopono is a little known but extremely powerful self-transformation technique.

Ho'oponopono originated from Hawaii and was originally taught by Morrnah Nalamaku Simeona. Morrnah was a healer, and in 1983 she received a great honor by being designated as a living treasure of Hawaii. She was teaching Ho'oponopono to small and large groups of people as well as to hospitals, colleges, and even to United Nations' personnel. She also founded the Foundation of I to promote principles of Ho'oponopono around the world.

Dr. Hew Len was the most avid student of Morrnah Simeona and a practitioner of updated Ho'oponopono technique. He was the first person who got documented and confirmed proof of the healing miracles initiated by the Ho'oponopono process. Dr. Hew Len observed Ho'oponopono healing powers when Morrnah Simeona healed his daughter from painful bleeding shingles (skin disease) that she suffered from for more than a decade without anyone or anything helping.

Dr. Hew Len improved and practiced updated Ho'oponopono processes every day, and these processes caused the most miraculous transformation within the most challenging environment, within three years.

From 1984 till 1987, he worked as a staff psychologist for Hawaii State Hospital, overseeing high-security unit housing criminally insane male patients. Now to make things clear, these are the type of guys you don't want to turn your back on. These guys committed murders, rapes, assaults, and due to their degree of "insanity" were locked into psychiatric high-security facility. Violence against each other and staff members were common.

So What Exactly Is Ho'oponopono and How Does It Work?

It is a tool for atonement, erasing effects of past actions, others, situations. It is a tool to use when you face any adversity situation.

When Joe Vitale met with Dr. Hew Len and asked him how exactly how he managed to heal these violent patients without actually seeing each of them in person, his answer was "I did not heal them. I healed part of myself that created them."

To me that was the most fundamental revelation to date. That phrase alone explains the most important presumption of Ho'oponopono: *You are 100 percent responsible for everything.* Everything and everywhere! And it means not only your personal screw ups and your personal successes. It means if someone somewhere did something and you became aware of that, you are 100 percent responsible for that.

Ho'oponopono is not your free ticket to guilt trip. Being 100 percent responsible is not the same as feeling infinitely guilty for miseries. It's a reminder of your creative powers and gentle welcome to return back to your inner nature. That is to zero. Joe Vitale wrote a great book on the subject called *zero limits*. When you're returning back to your most inner nature—to zero—everything becomes available to you effortlessly and you are being driven by inspiration from Divinity, not by petty ego wants. Ho'oponopono's zero is the same thing that Eckhart Tolle names *unmanifested*.

Back to practical reality—let's assume that zero is the next great thing after sliced bread. Or even before sliced bread.

How Do We Get to That "Magical" State? What Exactly Is Needed to Be Done?

This is achieved by constant cleaning process. Cleaning is the actual Ho'oponopono practice. Cleaning what? You clean yourself from subconscious garbage—programs that run your life without your participation.

Ho'oponopono process is very simple. Actual Ho'oponopono cleaning process consists of repetitions of the following phrases:

- I love you.
- Please forgive me.
- I am sorry.
- Thank you.

These phrases repeated will ignite the self-transformation process for the practitioner. This is exactly what Dr. Hew Len did to invite divine transformation powers for his surrounding during his work at Hawaiian mental hospital.

HOW TO LOSE WEIGHT: AN EFFECTIVE NATURAL METHOD WITH NO SIDE EFFECTS (ADAPTED FROM DR. DUKAN)

Remember to take your supplements every day.

This method is in four phases:

The First Phase

This is where you lose the most. You should lose around ½ to 1lbs per day.

During five days, only proteins and plain Greek yogurt are allowed. You must have both. You can eat as much as you want of both. Only natural proteins like chicken, turkey, fish, and eggs, but mostly white. Protein powders are not allowed and only organic tofu. No mayo, no oil, no ketchup, and no sugar of course. No alcohol or soda. Only tea, coffee, and nonfat milk are allowed. Forget the pork and the ham. No fruits or dessert, of course. The best is to buy from the deli slices of chicken and turkey.

Breakfast: tea or coffee, Greek yogurt, or two eggs
Lunch: chicken and yogurt
Diner: grilled salmon and Greek yogurt

The Second Phase

During five days, you will now eat some proteins and greens plus some yogurt. You can have all vegetables except all starches, avocado, white and red beans, rice, potatoes, lentils, and all peas. Still a lot of proteins, at least half and half proteins. Greens only 2 teaspoon of oil and only balsamic vinegar. You will repeat these two phases until you have reach the desired weight.

Please be responsible you do not want to have adverse effect. No more than 12 lbs at a time.

Third Phase (The Cruising Phase)

The duration will be of *ten days per pounds lost* (5 lbs × 10 = 50 days).

During this phase, you will not lose any weight, but it is a necessary phase if you do not want to gain any weight again.

Proteins and greens plus some yogurt.

*Every Thursday, only proteins.

*Sundays and Friday, anything you want that is not allowed (one desert or one drink), but only one time, lunch or dinner.

You are also allowed of two slices of all grain bread per day. One portion of banana, grapes, cherry, or dry fruits, the content of one small yogurt per day of pasta and one small portion of lamb one time during the week.

The Last Phase (Stabilizing Phase)

No more restrictions, only proteins day every Thursday for the rest of your life.

Claim Your Perfect Health, But Also Discover Your Purpose and Your Destiny

That will take you on an incredible voyage of inner discovery. You will see how it fits in perfectly with the natural flow of the universe and even with the original reason for life itself. Your journey of discovering is waiting.

The Human Body Is a Wonderful Matrix of Light and Color!

From our skin to our core, we are made of light, and light is the language by which our cells speak to one another. The DNA within the center of the nucleus of each cell of the body has been shown to emit *light*. And we resonate to the *sound frequency* too.

EXTRACT FROM THE BOOK OF KNOWLEDGE: THE KEYS OF ENOCH BY J. J. HURTAK

Key 3.1.7.9

The human evolution is preconditioned experiment within a world of happenstance relativity. Without higher evolutionary programming or direct programming by over self-intelligence, the human biological system must go back into overall flux of Magnetic fields when system is discorporate.

When Man is directly programmed by Overself, he is no longer kept in biochemical slavery within a three-dimensional consciousness by the "apparent realities of the earth." The Body is a grid magnetic domains which moves between the primary blueprint of the over self and the pattern angles of the human organs (the axial relationship).

The lines which tie together these magnetic domains are the axiatonal lines. The axiatonal lines can exist independent but still require the governing functions of the Higher Evolution. Man at this time, is being advanced to a new biological program of creation. If Man has to go into further soul progression he *must* connect his axiatonal lines to over self which is also making ascension into the next quantum level of Adam Kadmon, just as Adam Kadmon body is making ascension into a completely new program in our Son Universe.

Here, the Divine Father calls before Himself the unity that has been perfectly balanced between the body of the last Adam Kadmon and the spiritual-physical body of the first Adam Kadmon, before the collection of the Christ as the first and the last can offer up this eon to the father and pass into a new eon of the Living Light.

The physical creation is no longer separated from the divine Ain Soph, but is restored through the Christ Light penetrating the flesh, and the Divine Light penetrating the Overall so that both spiritual and physical bodies become one in sight of the Father. A whole species is being created at this time by the bringing together of the Academic Overself—human creation which allow this spiritual-biological expression of the Christ Race to be advanced to next consciousness time zone of creation.

Key 3.1.7.29

The axiatonal lines are parts of fifth-dimensional circulatory system combining Color and Sound, which are used to draw from the Overself-body basic energy used for the renewing function of the human evolutionary body.

Conversely, axiatonal lines operate prior to the action potential for the animation of the human species.

Furthermore, they bring together the all-important tonal vibrations governing each axis and all ultrasonic activities connected with the colors of healing that relate to each tone and multiple thereof.

The axiatonal network of the Shekina controls the geometric pressure fluctuations, which underline mechanisms controlling new mutations, and aids in the proper conversion of the chemistry of the human Light spectrum into wavelength forms of the higher evolution. Through the axiatonal arrangement, both acoustical vibrations of spiritual Light and sustaining Love are conveyed to the human system bringing the joy and Glory of the Living Light.

The Key then opens the door for sonic vibrations (sounds and ultrasound in crystalline structure) generating gravitational light within the body.

Key 3.1.7.33

The axiatonal lines can be used for the complete regeneration of an organ and even to resurrect dead, when activated by the proper energies. This key is to be used at the time when human evolutionary molecular grids are in direct alignment with the higher evolutionary resonance grid, permitting ultrasonic pulsations to allow for direct changes within vascular bodies.

ALLOPATHIC AND HOLISTIC MEDICINE

Allopathic, or conventional medicine, defines health as the absence of disease. And little emphasis is given to preventive treatment. Holistic (natural) medicine considers the human body to be the best form of resistance against and treatment for disease. When illness is present, holistic healing first acts to strengthen a person's natural resistance so he or she can face the disease with efficacy. Holistic medicine is considered a slow process in which results are experienced with time. This is because treatment of the entire person often requires lifestyle changes and deliberate therapies. Allopathic medicine also considers the main causes of illness to be pathogens, bacteria, viruses, or biochemical imbalances. To correct these problems, prescription drugs, radiation, or surgeries are often the recommended treatment. Then, patients suffer from the same maladies and repeat the cycle of diagnosis and medication. Holistic medicine provides patients with improved overall health.

Allopathic versus Holistic Medicine

In sharp contrast to the theories of allopathic medicine, holistic healing focuses on preventing illness before it begins. The mental, emotional, spiritual and physical aspects of a person are critical to the whole.

Whether physical or psychological, allopathic medicine ignores the why of illness and instead focuses on the question of how this can be remedied.

9.1.1. Complete Guide to Natural Healing

Holistic medicine uses combinational therapy to combat disease, bolster the body's own defenses. And, in turn, restores balance to a person.

In ancient Chinese medicine, doctors were paid only when patients were healthy. But in Western medicine, doctors are paid at the time of service for injury, disease, and illness.

WHAT IS AN IMMORTAL BODY OF LIGHT?

In the Judeo-Christian tradition, this body is called the resurrection body, or the glorified body, and Saint Paul named it the celestial body, or the spiritual body.

Spiritual realization has progressive phases of transformation. That is, very real and tangible physical changes occur as a person ascends in consciousness through mystical or transpersonal experiences. In the last stage of enlightenment, according to esoteric teaching in various traditions, the cells within the human body are changed from matter, flesh, into pure energy, light. Through the process of transubstantiation of the blood, skin, and bone, one actually transcends into a light being.

In Sufism, it is called the sacred body and the supracelestial body.

In Taoism, it is called the diamond body, and those few humans who have attained it are called the immortals.

The Tantrism and various Yoga systems, it is called the vajra body and the adamantine body.

In the Tibetan Buddhism, it is called the light body. In Egypt, it is was called the luminous being.

Sri Aurobindo, a great Indian teacher and mystic, declared that the *Divine body* is the ultimate goal of human evolution. He said dormant seeds of immortality exit within each of us now waiting to bloom and bear fruit. Thus as the caterpillar carries within its DNA genetic memory bank—called a genome—the blueprint for the butterfly, we have an unimaginable transformation event ahead of us as well. For we, too, are to be born again as diaphanous, translucent, butterfly-like being of light.

Indeed, only 3 percent of the three billion base pair genome of our DNA encodes for the construction of the physical body. Ninety percent of these DNA base pairs appear to be inactive during the normal course of human life. In heaven, shadow and darkness does not exist.

The human brain is the most complex yet powerful of the world, and yet we utilize only a small fraction of it. It only weighs 2 percent of your body's weight, but uses more than 20 percent of your body's energy.

And if you need to stimulate its clarity, boost your memory and focus, or increase your brain blood flow and its oxygen level and also eliminate mental foggy state, you should consider taking some ginkgo gotu kola (NSP has a very good one).

IS THERE A DIFFERENCE BETWEEN THE CHEMICAL COMPOSITION OF TEARS OF JOY AND THAT OF TEARS OF SADNESS?

Are there actually chemical differences in the tears?

"Happy tears" are made up of salt water and not a great deal else.

The "sad tears" were found to contain the very same chemicals and enzymes that are found in tumors, ulcers, and other such lumps and bumps and sicknesses throughout the body. The body, when crying in sadness, is literally flushing out all of the toxic chemicals that accumulate and are a part of the sadness / heart ache experience. Emotional tears contain many more than basal or irritant tears (crying with onions, your tear glands know the difference) of a certain important ingredient: proteins.

Emotional tears contain more proteins than "irritant" tears, the kind you shed while slicing onions.

All tears contain three chemicals released by the body during stress. They are the following:

- Leucine enkephalin—an endorphin believed to modulate pain sensation.
- ACTH—a hormone considered to be the body's most reliable indicator of stress .
- Prolactin—the hormone that regulates milk production in mammals.

Both emotional and irritant tears contain thirty times more manganese than is found in blood, suggesting that human tear glands can concentrate and remove substances from the body.

They are three kinds of tears, which differ from each other by function and also, probably, by composition.

Basal tears actually form continuously. Every time we blink, our eyelids spread the basal solution out over the surface of our eyeballs. Basal tears keep our eyes lubricated, important in preventing damage by air currents and bits of floating debris.

Basal tears, like all tears, have numerous components. A little bit of mucus allows them to adhere to the eye surface without causing harm. The main part of a tear contains, predictably, water and salts (like sodium chloride and potassium chloride).

Our eyes produce *irritant,* or reflex, *tears* when hit by wind or sand (or insects or rocks) and have the same constituents as basal tears and work toward the same goal: protecting the eyes. However, since they are designed to break down and eliminate eyeball intruders like airborne dust, these tears tend to flow in greater amounts and probably contain a greater concentration of antibodies and enzymes that target microorganisms. Thus, irritant tears are not just basal tears in greater quantity; different biological processes precede the excretion of the two types of solution.

Emotional tears—the voluminous tears that so rapidly move us to frustration or pity. Secreted in moments of intense feeling—sometimes *joy,* but more often *sorrow*—these tears aren't there to cleanse the eyes of irritating microbes or debris. The function of emotional tears can be inferred from their constituents. Emotional tears contain much more than basal or irritant tears of a certain important ingredient: proteins.

The proteins found in emotional tears are hormones that build up to very high levels when the body withstands emotional stress.

If the chemicals associated with stress did not discharge at all, they would build up to toxic levels that could weaken the body's immune system and other biological processes. But here, as in other areas, the body has its own mechanisms of coping. We secrete stress chemicals when we sweat and when we cry. Clearly, then it is physically very healthy to cry regardless of whether or not it feels awkward or embarrassing socially. The reason people will frequently report feeling better after a well-placed cry is doubtless connected to the discharge of stress-related proteins; some of the proteins excreted in tears are even associated with the experience of physical pain, rendering weeping a physiologically pain-reducing process. Tears produced during emotional crying have a chemical composition that differs from other types of tears. They contain significantly greater quantities of the hormones prolactin, adrenocorticotropic hormone, potassium, and manganese.

Crying is slightly differently. In temporal perspective, sorrowful crying is due to looking to the past with regret or to the future with dread. This illustrated crying as a result of losing someone and regretting not spending more time with them or being nervous about an upcoming event. Crying as a result of happiness would then be a response to a moment as if it is eternal—the person is frozen in a blissful, immortalized present.

YOUR JOURNEY BACK HOME

Let us talk about souls, in the world of duality, where everything is a relationship, and in the world of oneness, where everything is love.

There are different types of soul groups:

- *Union Souls*—they were birthed as one and were separated at the end of the density experience of Atlantis. They are seeking to reunify with their other soul half. They held a lifelong remembrance of another "half."
- Omni Souls—they have always remained as one experience of the light. They are complete without a partner, being in fullness with the Divine always. Omni souls make ideals nuns and monks.
- Dual Soul—similar to twins. Different from union soul. They are individuals yet find greater Divine communion with their counterpart. Often confused with the union soul. Dual souls are looking for their cosmic twin who, when found, may even look physically alike.
- Multi-expressional soul—these souls have always embodied many expressions of light and seek to incorporate all expressions. They integrate all of their experience. It is their way of bringing all experiences back to the Divine.

All of these Soul groups are returning to their wholeness with the source now. They are reunifying back into pure soul-group expression.

What About You?

Yes! You do have a choice! You can claim your mastery. Many choices are made along the path. Many are the habit of the habit of the pain.

How often have you felt you were missing something? How often have you felt you are doing wrong, that you needed help? How often have you felt confused, depressed, tired, or lonely?

With the beginning of the ascension, you have to take action.

You are writing your road map as you go, and it is time to bring your complete cocreative power and intuitive wisdom.

Let us awaken all to our highest potential now! There is *urgency*. We are at the time of reunion.

Are you ready to take the steps required to ascend?

Are you ready to be reconnected to your higher-self, your Angel?

Are you ready to heal your body to regenerate and rejuvenate?

KARMA

Let us talk about karma a little bit now. The definition of karma is the quality of somebody's current and future lives as determined by that person's behavior in this and previous lives.

The release of the karmic imperative means that all debts are forgiven and all contracts are complete and everyone is free to be fully responsible for their actions. With it comes great responsibility. This is the tremendous shift in consciousness if you allow it in.

"You are eternally shifting, moving, and creating anew, over and over again. What a gift, the ability to continually expand. This is a process that cannot be terminated for you cannot terminate expansion! It can only renew itself. Know that even when you feel as you are in a phase when you are expanding, you are renewing!

"Within the traditional system, the crown chakra is at the top of the head. As the ascended state of the Divine galactic blueprint, your crown chakra is three points of energy. The top is six inches above your head, and then there is one to the right and one to the left. Together they form the base of a pyramid of energetic light that includes your third eye and these three points. These are the four points of the base.

"The root of this system is your heart chakra, which is the two Divine intersecting spirals of emerald green and gold. Move to the *truth* chakra (former throat chakra), which is an aquamarine. It is beautiful emerald green that comes up and meets with that, which was formerly blue, and turns into aquamarine, thereby offering great truth and connectivity.

"Next you have the third eye, which is an opalescent pearl of two Divine intersecting infinity swirls. From here, go six inches above the head to discover the top of the new crown, which also has a point to the right and a point to the left. It's like a helmet.

"Understand that helmet brings you into great lifting energy. It is very important that you no longer have all that activity going on in those first three chakras." (Sri Ram Kaa and Angelic Oracle Kira Raa, 2012)

EFT AND HTP

Emotional Freedom Therapy EFT

Founded by Gary Craig, the Emotional Freedom Technique, or EFT, is the psychological acupressure technique recommended to optimize your emotional health. It is based on the same energy meridians used in traditional acupuncture to treat physical and emotional ailments but without the invasiveness of needles, instead simple tapping of the fingertips. This combination of tapping the energy meridians and voicing positive affirmation works to clear the emotional block from your body's bioenergy system, thus restoring your mind and body's balance, which is essential for optimal health and the healing of physical disease.

EFT is very easy to learn and will help you

- remove negative emotions
- reduce food cravings (weight loss)
- reduce or eliminate pain
- implement positive goals

Advanced HPT—Heart Point Technique
The Fabulous New Healing Modality Directly from the Divine Mother to Rebecca, a Messenger That Says to Be Blessed in Service (http://rebeccamarina.com/hpt)

HPT is a brand-new healing modality that works by harnessing the power of spirit with the wonderful energy of the heart.

It says that you must cover somebody's points with your hand or fingertips.

The great thing about heart point techniques is that it combines the very best of energy healing techniques with Divine guidance. HPT does work on a spiritual and energetic basis and gives clarity to any situation that needs healing.

Heart point techniques can help you to

- attract more money
- attract more love
- build an energy healing business
- heal your emotional, physical body
- become a healer or enhance your skills

The energetic points are the following:

1. *The higher self-point*—eighteen to twenty-four inches above the head. The HSP is a gateway to all the divine intelligence and assistance that you could ever need.
2. *The crown point*—right on the very top of the head. Four meridians come together here. The corpus callosum, a thick bundle of nerves, runs through here as well. The corpus callosum separates the right and left halves of the brain and helps the R/L hemispheres communicate.
3. *The Third Eye*—the seat of your intuition. Also key in stimulating the hypothalamus, pineal gland, and supporting organs.

    In addition to this, you can cover the whole of the eye points with your hand, and you will be covering the emotional centers, the center for fear, and the points where all acupressure meridians enter the brain.
4. *The heart point*—Cradle the heart slightly to the left. Your heart is not right in the center. The heart itself is a powerful source of intelligence and healing.
5. *The consolidation point*—This is at the base of the head, the occipital point. When tapping here, you are sending

messages up into the brain and down into the spine and nervous system at the same time.

The first time you do HPT, it is recommended to "touch, bless, and give permission to open" for each point. Simply touch the point and say, "I bless you and give you permission to open."

In the early fall season I was on my way to the grocery store and parked my car when I saw a man walking towards me with a great smile. He aproached me and said:
"I am here to give you some important information. As you already know there is recovery through understanding the true root causes of symptoms, fears and dependencies. There is no need to use dangerous drugs, or any shots and to be stuck anymore. The holistic approach is the way and you know it very well. "
The next thing I know I had the vision of Archangels knocking on my door saying,
"The people of Earth are being offered a chance to join the rest of the universe in peace and participate in spiritual awakening.
What's behind the suppress awareness of the energy healing power to the public?
On average two disease outbreak events every week are identified by a surveillance team, and the context in which these events occur is far more complex than before. Energy healing is much more effective than chemical healing, the drugs, pills without any side effects.
What if the coronavirus is "a wake-up call? If the new vaccines were a technology that is damaging the DNA and disrupting cells metabolism? If it was lowering your immune system and some persons had some terrible side effects from it?
When you as human beings realize that you are not your thoughts and emotions, you get a whole new clarity. The world becomes much brighter. All the knowledge you need is inside of you, it's just blocked by your thoughts and emotions. Like the fear.

All of the answers are already inside of you. If you get yourself quiet enough to get in contact with that knowledge, your clarity will come flooding back.

It is there waiting for you.

Then I saw in vision that a man had the covid, and no doctor would take him in. He met an Holistic Practitioner and discovered the E.F.T. and a breathing technique taping on specific points of the face. And the man said this breathing technique helped me get the last of my Covid Cough under control!

That's how he did it:

Emotional Freedom Therapy and a breathing technique to control your Covid Cough

Tap the side of your hands: (karate chop) Even though I have some constricted breathing I completely love and accept myself. (3 times side of hands.)

Then each points constricted breathing.

Relax and take deep breath.

Now ask yourself and say outloud: What would we have than constricted breating? Deeper fully breaths

Then side of hands 3 times tap: I still have constricted breathing, I chose to allow my lung to open up more fully.

Top of the head in little round around tap and say I chose to allow my lung to open up more fully.

Inner corner of the eye tap and say: Lungs open up fully
side of the eye: tap and say: Lungs open up
Underneath the eye tap and say: breathing deeply
Under the nose: relaxing and breathing deeply
under the lip: Under the nose: I'm chosing to breath more fully
on the collar bone: I'm chosing to breath more fully
Under arm pit: I'm chosing to breath more fully
Relax and take another breath again

Now start commanding your body. Your physiology will pay attention to open up now.

Top of the head: Lungs open up
Inner corner of the eye: Lungs open up
Side of the eye: Sway deep breath
Underneath the eye: Lungs open up
Under the nose: I'm feeling really good
Under the lip: I'm tingling all over
On the collar bone: Lungs open up
Under arm pit: I'm feeling really good.

THE LIVING ANKH PRACTICE

This practice is done in two steps. It is important to first run the energy up your feet and out the top of your head, and then out through your hands. (Sri Ram Kaa and Angelic Oracle Kira Raa, 2012)

- Begin by standing.
- Visualize a white ray of light coming into your left foot and up the left leg, and visualize a golden ray of light entering your right foot and up your right leg.
- These rays meet at the base of your spine, where they intertwine at each of the traditional chakras. This intertwining will give you the visual effect of the caduceus, an ancient symbol that has been commonly adopted by medical doctors.
- Send this blended energy stream all the way up and out the crown.
- After you have established this energy flow from the feet up, then call in an emerald beam from the universe right into your heart chakra. Extend your arms to each side and send the energy out each arm and then through each palm chakra.
- See the energy blend with the golden white spiral, and then ask it to flow out your palms. Extend your hands outward as far as you are able, and call in an ever-greater flow.

Egyptian hieroglyph on the cross means "holy writings." Ankh is the key symbol for eternal life. Ankh means "life" and it represents union of heaven and earth "Oneness" and interdimensional communication.

The *ankh* is one of the primary key symbols in Egyptian times. There is an electromagnetic energy in energy field surrounding our bodies shaped like the ankh. The remembrance of it, according to the Egyptian, is the beginning of our returning home to *eternal life* and the *freedom*, so the *ankh* is the primary key. It represents leaders, the one who has power of decision and responsibility.

And we are, CHADD and VIE, the keepers of the secret contained in his hands.

The Great Pyramid is a cosmic tool and has zero gravity inside the king's chamber (double square unable)

It was built seventeen thousand years ago and by levitation/anti-gravitation (trans-substantiation). At that time, they were much more advanced than us. We have lost the ability; we have forgotten the knowledge of levitation. It is such a very important tool for us. What we know as the Crystal Palace is called a *Dogo*.

SACRED GEOMETRY

Geomancers are interested in *sacred geometry* because this is the study of the way that spirit integrates into matter by echoing and amplifying the geometry of nature and planetary movements. We help to align the resonance of body, mind, and spirit with the harmonic frequencies of the above and the below. Circle is *yin* and the spiritual realms. Square is *yang* and being the physical world.

Geomancers are interested in s*acred geometry* because it has been found that certain spaces, with particular ratios, enable the participant to resonate or vibrate at the appropriate rate that maximizes the possibility of connection to the One (double square to go back to one).

Understanding How Light and Sound Therapy and Sacred Geometry Unlock Your Healing

The geometry is a mathematic science that studies the relations between points, right curved, surfaces, and volumes of space, and when one adds to its consciousness, and the opening of the heart, it becomes sacred geometric forms. The forms of geometry are the mirror of our conscious; to open it allows realizing that the geometry is the base of any life on ground and in our universe.

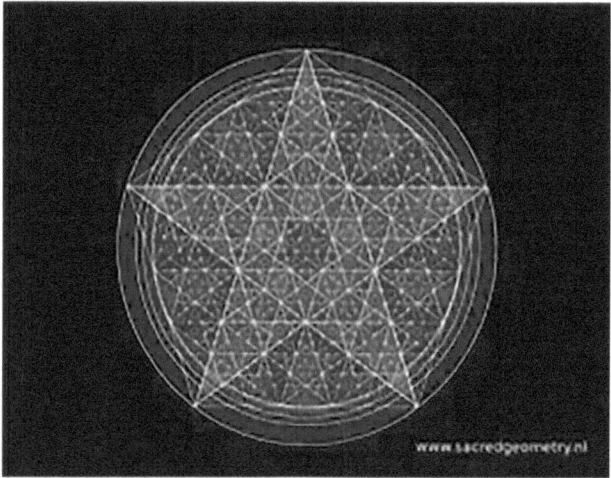

Geometry can enable us to remember our origins, to be helped to cure on the emotional planes, intellectual or physical. It shows us that we are all interconnected and that we can perceive the various existing planes of conscience.

The flower of life is the form that hides the secrecy of any form of life on ground and in this universe. By looking at it, we see various geometrical forms including five solids of Plato that are overlapping one another. When they are studied, it is realized that nature is divisible and holographic. One finds it in many countries and as well sure in Egypt in the large pyramid. Beside it one sees also forty-seven other diagrams, one behind the other, representing the chromosomes of the Christique consciousness, levels toward which one moves now.

Before we can heal ourselves, we first need to be cleaned.

We need to purify ourselves to prepare us for our own individual transition.

A powerful way of doing this is by using sacred geometry. Science has proven long ago that our bodies are geometrically designed systems. Our subconscious recognizes complex sacred geometrical *symbols* that have been used since time immemorial.

Although our conscious minds will not understand, and even might think them strange, sacred geometry has a powerful effect on our mental state and also our physical body and even more powerful when added to a light and sound treatment. When the light reaches the crystalline structure of the cell wall, it is greatly amplified.

The light radiates from the cell and naturally congregates with like cells because they share the same frequency (color) of light. These groups of cells form organs and the other structures in our body, each resonating with a *specific color.*

Now, *imagine* if you could actually change your blueprint of life. *Imagine* if you woke up one day and realized that you had dormant superhuman abilities that were waiting to be unleashed and that perfect health awaits you.

Mother Earth's Crystal Grid System Functions Just Like Our Acupuncture Meridians

Earth's crystal grid system is the system that functions within the body of Mother Earth in the same way humanity's chakras, acupuncture meridians, and acupuncture points function in our bodies. The crystal grid system is the vehicle through which the light of God is flowing to increase the energy, vibration, and consciousness of every atomic and subatomic particle and wave of precious life energy to exist on earth. Each acupuncture meridian is represented within the acupuncture pressure points in our hands. We receive and transmit energy through our hands, and the light flowing through our acupuncture meridians is the life force. It nourishes and sustains every gland, muscle, cell, organ, and function of our physical body. It allows us to live, breathe, move, and think. The light we receive through our hands flows through every acupuncture meridian and help to unblock the areas in our body.

Meridian Lines—Originally, the meridian lines (also called acupuncture lines) on our bodies were connected to the grid lines that encircle the planet and cross at acknowledged power places such as Machu Picchu and Sedona. These grid lines were designed to continue out and connect us to a vastly larger grid, tying us into the entire universe. This interface is a channel that facilitates our communication of energy, light, and information between large and small, macrocosm and microcosm, the universe and humankind. At one point in time, we became disconnected from these lines and lost the fullness of our inherent connection to the universe, distancing us from our previously rapid and expansive rate of evolution. The reconnection brings in *new* axiatonal lines that reconnect us on a more powerful and evolved level lines than ever before. These lines are part of a timeless network of intelligence, a parallel-dimensional system that draws the basic energy for the renewal functions of the human body. Meridian lines are reactivated, allowing for the exchange, beyond energy, of light and informing the reconnection of DNA strands and the reintegration of strings (simultaneously occurring, or parallel, planes of existence). Although science currently sees human DNA as a two-strand double helix, there are many, many more strands that exist within our multidimensional structure waiting to be reconnected. Blood and DNA are cleansed; blocks and emotions are released for the ever.

9.1.1. Complete Guide to Natural Healing

It then removes the energetic blockages, allowing embodiment of your higher self, the part of you closest to Source, or God. Expansion of your consciousness is one of the main benefits; you will simply become more aware, especially what your purpose is and why you incarnated here at this point in time. You will start to become aware or see things that others cannot see—some of the hidden agendas going on and how to make decisions to help you and your family in the best way possible. Your dormant brain functions will start to become active, especially your pineal gland. Some of the physical benefits reported include increased energy and rejuvenation of various muscles. You will start to see how your body is just a thought form as well, and you can change your body more easily with focus, so you won't have to work out as much. Your body will undergo a detoxification, which will bring old emotional issues to the surface to be released forever, to no longer cause disease and poison the body. Almost everyone also reports much quicker manifestations of that which they desire.

"The Secret" of Therapeutic Light of the Spectrum That We Use, Plus Biosound Frequency and Sacred Geometric Forms and All Combined, Access Healing

Let's explain: Disease on any level—physical, mental, soul, or spiritual—is incorrect vibratory rate(s) patterns that are not appropriate or blocked energy pathway(s) within, or even between, the various levels of existence.

The geometrical amplifiers used here, in combination with the spectra-light, has the ability to balance human energy fields and contains a complex informational system that can be used to access healing in various fields of healing using the matrix of information to explore and better understand.

This is the most all-inclusive form of all therapies. Each color and sound is a specific vibratory rate and also works in harmonics intervals with other rates. And can thus be used to return/reeducate diseased bodies, emotions, and thoughts too.

The Importance of Geometric Forms

The forms of geometry are the mirror of our conscience. Geometry can enable us to remember our origins, to be helped to cure on the emotional planes, intellectual or physical. It shows us that we are all interconnected and that we can perceive the various existing plans of conscience.

We Are Holographic Bodies of Light

Science has proven long ago that our bodies are geometrically designed systems. Our subconscious recognizes complex sacred geometrical symbols that have been used since time immemorial. Although our conscious minds will not understand, and even might think them strange, sacred geometry has a powerful effect on our mental state and also our physical body.

In our institute sessions, we use a light that operates on 2.4 V light bulb (a gentle approach to address subtle energy pattern) and equipped with superior mineral-based crystalline quality color filters. Each filter provides 80 percent *faster energy* transmission compared to LEDs (LED contain mercury and arsenic) or plastic filters. Specific source with crystalline colors of the spectrum, which are wavelength and frequency, and biosound to balance energy wherever body is lacking it and to remove blockages and applied to specific meridian points. Our bodies have meridians carrying energy and connecting with each organ, and all organs correspond to a specific color. When blockages in meridians happen, disease follows. Healing then takes place on a wide spectrum and levels: physical, mental, emotional, and spiritual.

"As we embrace the state of Divine Union, our chakras flow as balanced, infinite spirals. The state of non-attachment allows energy to rise and center in the heart, offering connection with true peace, love and joy" (Sri Ram Kaa and Kira Raa, 2012).

THE IMPORTANCE OF THE CHAKRAS

The word *chakra* means "wheel" in Sanskrit (East Indian). Chakras are energy vortices. There are many chakras in your body, but there are seven main best well-known.

A more accurate translation would be "spinning wheel." Chakras are different-colored energy centers that originate throughout the body, from seven different points that are responsible for the conditions of your mind, body, and spirit. The wheels are meant to spin in the same direction, at the same speed, all at the same time. When we have blockages in our body, the wheels slow down or sometimes stop at various points in the body, hence problems can arise.

When functioning well, the chakras are thought to be a conduit for the constant flow of energy throughout our bodies. If these chakras are blocked, slowed in their spinning, darkened, or not working, then you can correct this imbalance by imagining them being cleared from negative energies such as resentment, fear, or trauma. Tuning up your chakras can make an enormous difference to your sense of well-being in general as they conduct the natural flow of energy through our bodies. Chakras that are blocked are thought to cause physical disease and emotional and spiritual disease. Common blockages are negative emotions, the desire to hurt, being emotionally hurt, and the holding on to of fears and resentment and sometimes past life issues. The chakras interact with each other in a constant dancing of the spheres that extends outside our bodies. They exist in a constant state of renewal that can be enhanced by meditation, creative visualization, light working, and breath work. Thanks to 8/8/8 that was the opening of the Orion, we can now activate our eight chakras.

Regardless of your understanding of the chakra system, we all understand love. Love heals, unifies, encourages, expands, and nourishes us. The intention of this is to offer you an expanded paradigm and to help you anchor in your heart. When we truly anchor our hearts, new responses to perceive problems arise automatically. True harmony results!

The Seven Chakras

It is the channel of *universal healing*. The health aura and the body receive energy from higher levels via energy vortices, the chakras, which are as spinning antennas rooted in the spine or glands in the head.

There are the seven major chakras, "energy wheels," which correspond to and are activated by the seven colors of the rainbow. Their correlations are as follows:

- Red—root chakra
- Blue—throat chakra
- Orange—sacral chakra
- Indigo—brow chakra
- Yellow—solar plexus chakra
- Violet—crown chakra
- Green—heart chakra
- White—perfect color blend

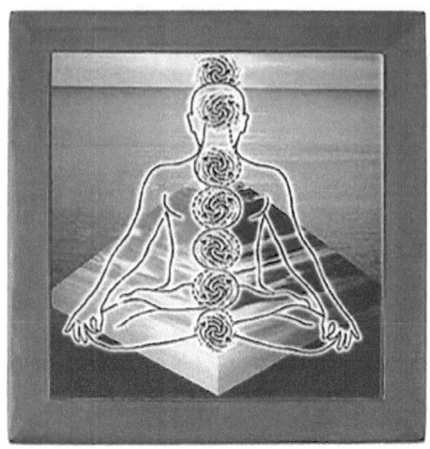

How Destructive Rays Weaken the Body

Just as improper polarity can distort the functions of a TV set, so can our bodies be damaged by improper vibrations (food or drugs), especially from outside the visible spectrum (X-rays and microwaves, for example).

When Balancing the Chakra

Chakras are the seven spinning energy centers of the human body that control every dimension of our physical, mental, and spiritual well-being. When each organ and energy vortex in your body (chakras) is balanced, blood and DNA are refreshed, dissolving toxins and blocks.

Chakras are our nonphysical organs.

Chakras are invisible organs in our body, but they support our physical organs with life. The closest way of describing this connection is by explaining the function of glands and hormones.

Each chakra is directly connected to a gland, and glands are organs in our body that produce hormones. Hormones are carriers flowing in our bloodstream that tells the cells what to. Any change that needs to be done in our body requires hormones to tell the cells to do so, and the immune system itself is depending on glands.

When chakras are dormant, they are unable to support their corresponding gland.

When a person is balanced, all chakras are active; all glands are balanced and healthy.

Chakras explain why the human form is nourished by light only and all else causes aging and, in the end, death.

Our body is much more than what our eyes tell us. Chakras are like the nonphysical organs. Chakras are like organs in our energy flow, and there is an entire energy flow in our body, though we can't see it.

They are placed along a vertical line. Chakras support the energy flow of the body.

The chakras support our body with energy. *Chakra* means "wheel" in Sanskrit. The stronger the intensity is, the brighter and stronger the chakra is. They also have their own specific body parts and organs as well as nonphysical aspects to maintain with life— nonphysical aspects being, for example, emotions and perception, understanding and consciousness.

The human form has great potential of awareness but only use a small percentage of their brains. Some people seems to begin to be able to use the other parts of it such as telepathy, though many people are unable or lack the ability of being in touch with their thoughts, intuition, or emotions as most people do not have all chakras active.

Each chakra has increasingly advanced functions starting from the red and up to the violet. They support the functions of the body. When a person is unconscious of the aspects that come with a chakra, that particular chakra is weaker or even dormant.

Red chakra is the basic one through which it gives us the wanting to survive, the hunger, of finding food, reproduction, physical instincts, taking care of our offspring.

Orange chakra is active in every human. In this we find creativity. Make the person understand that their action has affected the world.

Yellow chakra is not always active. But when open, the orange chakra, humans are now able to feel uncertain, anxious, afraid.

The *green chakra,* when it is activated, means that the person has reached a deeper emotional understanding of oneself and of others. For the ones with perfectly activated green chakras, they are able to feel love but also the pain when love is not there.

Blue chakra is most of the time weak in people. This fact has got to do with the way our society is and what we usually expect people to be and not be. Blue chakra is also related to communication.

The *indigo chakra* is related to intuition, spiritual abilities, and our senses, physical senses. We discover that we are immortal souls.

Violet chakra is the link to God, the source from which we came. With this active, there are no limits anywhere. We are connected to all existence, to God, and when this chakra is activated, it changes from violet to white.

Chakras support bodily functions because the wavelength of a color, for example, green, equals the wavelength of an occurrence such as emotions. All things have an energy aspect; all things have an auric color aspect. A color equals a wavelength and sound, and it also equals a material such as chemical substances.

- *Red*—Weak or imbalanced red chakra is rare.
- *Orange*—The orange chakra relates to our knowing that our actions affect the outside world.
- *Yellow*—This chakra is related to the outside world affecting us.
- *Green*—Feeling unloved or hated, and it makes the green turn dark.

- *Blue—Affects the thymus gland, which requires the support of the throat chakra. It sometimes results in various problems ranging from severe fatigue and weak immune system.*
- *Indigo—Mental illnesses.*
- *Violet/white—Always balanced.*

The reason we have seven chakras is related to seven dimensions and existence. It is also related to light and to God.

All things exist within white light or God. We are all of our organs and cells and tissue, and we have a conscious mind, but our organs are parts of our body. And so are the cells, being parts of organs. Cells function on their own, and one single cell does not even look like an organ or a human being, but they function on their own, function together in a blood stream, or tissue.

But to make it more complicated, we have more than the seven main chakras.

The *pink chakra* is smaller in size and supports the ability of unconditional love.

The "back of the head chakra," corpus callosum, is a chakra beyond chakra 7. It powers functions in the brain and perception. This chakra is white such as the active seventh chakra.

Feet chakras are black, they are low, sometimes no vibration, and enable the foundations of a body.

Hand chakras are located in the palms of our hands and usually of a red color but can differ in color, and they are the healing chakras. The healer can balance or correct an imbalance.

Higher chakras continue at the vertical of the seven main chakras. Higher chakras color is turquoise.

The seven chakras are of the larger in size.

When chakras are non-active, they cannot support their corresponding bodily functions. Healthy people have a strong flow of energy. People who are sick, weak, or dying have a weaker energy flow like dead bodies have no energy flow.

There is energy at the base of our spine, called the kundalini. But very few people have an active kundalini.

When the individual has reached the understanding for each of the seven chakras, the kundalini awakens and the powerful flow of energy runs up the spine, through each of the chakras, and reaches the seventh violet one, turning this chakra white.

Blocked chakras affect our energy and cause diseases.

Did You Know That Blocking the Chakra Also Prevent Enlightenment?

Root chakra is kept blocked by keeping us obsessed by degrading and sleazy sex, low morality sex, and pornography.

The *illusion* of freedom in the sexual arena creates the separation of sexual energy from the energy of the heart and from the crown center and thus splits the individual in a way that increasingly departs from the sacred. Sexual darkness has led and continues to lead to abuses of many kinds, to sexually transmitted diseases, and to a variety of dysfunctional relationship patterns.

The Return to Sacred Sexuality, Purification, and Sexual Scandals by Julie Redstone

The freedom to express impulses cannot be true freedom unless it takes into account one's whole being and especially one's heart in relation to the whole being and heart of another. Such freedom enhances the growth of each one and allows God to enter the relationship since the heart's love is fully present.

To begin with, freedom is not necessarily the capacity to do anything one wants with one's body. Sexual darkness has led and continues to lead to abuses of many kinds, to sexually transmitted diseases, and to a variety of dysfunctional relationship patterns. The separation of sexual energy from the energy of the heart and from love for God creates a desanctifying of the body, which is meant to become a sacred vessel of light. Particularly at this time, when light is expanding on the earth, such a desanctification is significant. As this takes place, both the embodied self and the human collective self can hold less light and bring less light to others. The choice for sacredness cannot happen when the body is used in pursuit of activities that satisfy only a portion of the self or when one part of the self remains separated from another part in order to pursue *ambitions* that do not foster wholeness and growth. For a return to the sacred can only happen through the affirmation that each one makes to do so, and through the willingness that each one expresses to hold the entire self—body, heart, and mind—as inextricably linked to the spiritual essence that lives at one's core.

How to Tell the Difference between Lust and Love by Dr. Judith Orloff

Pure lust is based solely on Physical attraction (Looks and Body) and fantasy--it often dissipates when the "real person" surfaces!!! To differentiate pure lust from love.

Signs of Lust

- You're totally focused on a person's looks and body. You're interested in having sex.
- You'd rather keep the relationship on a fantasy level.

Signs of Love

- You want to spend quality time together other than sex. You get lost in conversations and forget about the hours passing.
- You want to honestly listen to each other's feelings, make each other happy.

- He or she motivates you to be a better person.
- You want to get to meet his or her family and friends.

Other Ways You Chakra Is Being Blocked

1. Spleen—by food additives, pesticides, MSG, etc.
   More than one-third of all personal care products contain at least one ingredient linked to *cancer*. Parabens in nail lotion and shampoos. Phthalates in nail polish, shampoos, deodorant, and lotion. Coal tar in hair color and medicated shampoos. Triclosan in antibacterial soap, shampoo, facial cleanser, toothpaste, and deodorant. Sunscreen chemicals in sunscreens. Petroleum byproducts in lotions.
   Derivative of petroleum in lotion, lead and mercury in hair color, wound treatments, and artificial tears.
   Propellant made from petroleum processing in moisturizer, shaving cream, foot spray, and breath freshener. In skin, hair *conditioner. Hydroquinone in skin whitener. Nanoparticles in sunscreens and lotions.*
2. Solar plexus—by keeping us in a state of fear and negativity (horror and violence on TV, drugs)
3. Heart—lack of love
4. Throat—by the inability to speak out the truth, lack of freedom of expression.
5. Third eye or brow chakra—when it gets calcified by *fluoride!*

Gay people are lacking of the color yellow. They should wear yellow and eat some yellow food.

Chakra healing and color healing are the most effective form of healing.

Each chakra is directly connected to a gland; it's a nonphysical organ that supports our physical life. And glands are organs in our body that produce hormones. Hormones are carriers flowing in our bloodstream that tells the cells what to. Any change that needs to be done in our body requires hormones to tell the cells to do so, and the immune system itself is depending on glands.

When chakras are dormant, they are unable to support their corresponding gland.

When a person is balanced, all chakras are active, all glands are balanced and healthy, and adequate amounts of hormones are produced. This is why consciousness makes a person immortal.

THE PINEAL GLAND

In Ancient Egypt, it was symbolized by the Eye of Horus. It is considered the seat of the soul. It is located in the geometric center of the cranium. The pineal gland is about the size of a pea and is in the center of the brain in a tiny cave, behind and above the pituitary gland, which lies a little behind the root of the nose. It is located directly behind the eyes, attached to the third ventricle.

It is a very important organ that connects you to the higher reality, in which you experience spirituality. This gland happens to be the organ that regulates melatonin, thus regulates the times you're up and the times you're asleep.

So it appears the ancients knew full well the purpose and power of the pineal gland. Essentially it is the organ that separates our waking life from our sleeping life. Or our spiritual life, only one-sixtieth of the soul stays in the body during sleep, from our physical life. It's our umbilical cord to the higher world. This organ is also where we visualize or see things with our minds eye, considered the third eye, our inner vision, and the seat of the soul.

This gland is activated by light, and it controls the various biorhythms of the body. Specific usage of a specific geometric form in combination with the specific color frequency as well as the specific frequency of the sound can activate it to its fullest reconnection.

It works in harmony with the hypothalamus gland, which directs the body's thirst, hunger, sexual desire, and the biological clock, which determines our aging process. When the pineal gland awakens, one feels a pressure at the base of the brain. This pressure will often be experienced when connecting to a higher frequency. A head injury may also activate the third eye—pineal gland.

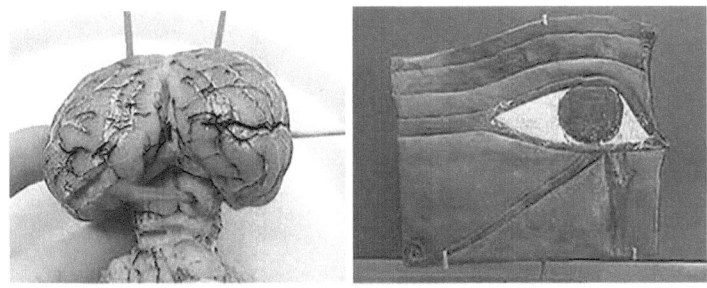

How Could He See and Drive though He Was Blind?

Well, blind people demonstrate that kind of ability.

When you're faced with that situation, you have the ability to project a sensing beam from your third eye area, and you can also sense from your hands. (You can actually sense from any chakra, but usually do it from the third eye or the hands.) You can project a beam of consciousness into a dark room for a certain distance. It might go only an inch, or maybe you can feel outward a foot or two, and you just know that nothing (or something) is in that space. Your consciousness goes out this distance, and then it stops and feels all around.

We actually have six of these sensing rays, not just one, but six. They all come from the center of our heads, the pineal gland. One ray comes out the front of our head at the third eye and another goes out the back; one goes out of the left and another out of the right side of our brain; and another goes straight up through the crown chakra and the sixth straight down through our neck—the six directions. These are the same directions of the x-y-z axes of geometry.

We have long forgotten the skills and abilities that the consciousness of the physical body carries. But we can communicate with it.

WHAT IS AURA

Everyone has an aura, and everyone has already seen or experienced the auric fields of others.

Children are very good at seeing and experiencing the aura. Those experiences are often translated into their drawings. Around the figures, they will shade in unusual and different colors. These colors often reflect the subtle energies they have observed around what they are drawing. This also plays an important part in your well-being. Your auric fields *must be kept clean of entities and stress.*

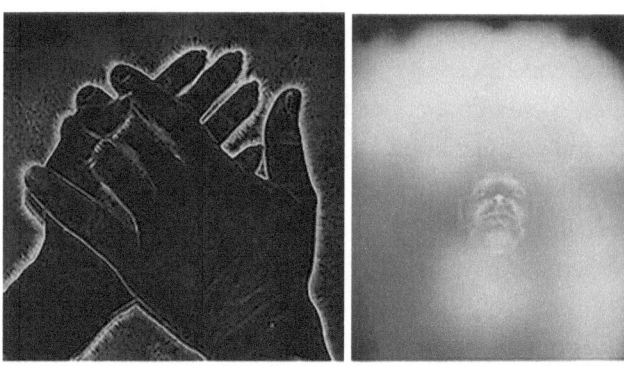

Phosphénisme/Phosphenism (Orb)

Phosphenism develops what is truly important to an individual as a priority. It helps the best in everyone to bloom through a harmonious originality expressed by *creativity*.

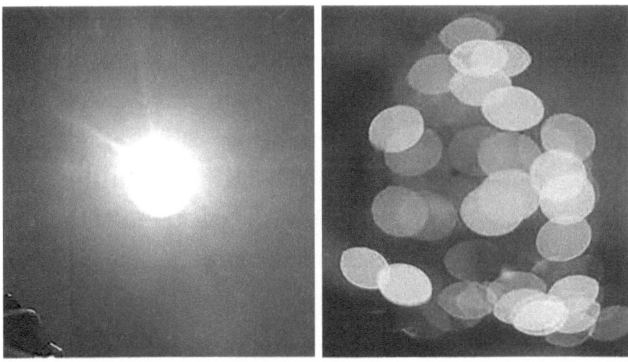

Individuals can be compared to the crystals of snow, which are all different, though all the angles that compose their patterns are sixty-degree angles. There is a relationship between the collective and the individual. The collective aspect is represented by the sixty-degree angles, which are common to all the crystals of snow. Each crystal has its own shape and harmony though, and these correspond to the individual aspect.

Phosphenism respects the collective structure while developing individual tendencies. The method is the same for everyone: mixing a thought with the phosphine, but the result is completely individual. Phosphenism helps the development of the best part of the individual and the blooming of a harmonious originality that is called creativity.

In 1959, a French doctor discovered and analyzed the action instigating of the light on all the cerebral functions. Its method is founded on *phosphines,* the multicolored spots that persist in darkness. The extraordinary one discovered of this French doctor is that the mixture of a thought to phosphine transforms luminous energy into mental energy. Phosphines then cause the development of the memory, the intelligence, the attention, the creativity, and the intuition. The application of the method is really simple pleasant; the progress and the results feel some quickly fast improvement. The child learns more quickly, retains its lessons, and is more attentive in class. The effects are felt as of the first meeting, with an increase in the capacities of attention and comprehension.

In Portugal, to improve the teaching method, tests of attention were made on groups of children, before and after the meetings of mixing phosphoric. Thus it was confirmed that this faculty is better after each meeting and that by the repetition of those during a few weeks, the improvement of the attention persists between the meetings.

Specific problems like *dyslexia* can be corrected as well as the problems of learning difficulties (they are in facts gifts). The students realize that the assimilation is faster and that the action is felt on comprehension. The ideas are structured better. The people who need to resume their studies after a long intellectual idle period will check quickly that their concentration is better, that they retain more matters better and that they work more quickly.

What You Must Know about Indigo's Profiles

They are highly intelligent in their own way. They are wired differently than other people. Indigos know in their heart and core that they are here on a mission, but many don't remember what that is.

They have an inner awareness that what is being taught in churches and schools is absolutely *not* accurate and know there are hidden agendas around the lies that are being accepted by the masses as truth. This is extremely frustrating for them, but they have a strong sense of ethics, justice, freedom, and truth. And it is why authority figures often irritate them. They will give their all for their cause and feel they would rather die than give in to tyranny and deception.

Most have strong and unusual psychic and telekinetic abilities and shut down psychic abilities because it scares people. Many times they get along better with animals and nature than humans as indigos have a bond connection to the trees and nature and can relate well to children and the elderly.

They would prefer sitting on the floor in school when they can. And many times they get very impatient with someone who doesn't get to the point. They have an innate sense of *oneness* and connectedness to all of creation. They get confused and disturbed when others don't share their reality. They have high capacity for love, and others may feel uncomfortable by their intensity.

Indigos are hyper sensitive and have an immense amounts need of physical touching, hugs, and love.

Indigos are labeled "dyslexic" and find themselves in special classes at school that usually never work for them.

Indigos have a strong desire to know why and, if they don't see the point in something or if it isn't explained properly, will feel it is simply not worth their time and energy and they will react with resistance.

Indigos have their own ways of calculation innately and many have been accused of cheating in school. They have an evolved awareness of how things work in Math, English, and Physics.

Indigos have a gift of healing whether it is hands on healing, healing with music and tone, or they have telepathic healing abilities. Because of their expanded perception, unusual creativity, and running way ahead of what is being taught in class, many were diagnosed as having *attention deficit disorder* and put on Ritalin as children.

Because of their feeling so foreign to this planet, a very high percentage of indigos have been put on also on antidepressants to make them appear "normal" and fit in our society. This is just a temporary fix though and only adds to their challenges.

Because of their feeling so out of place here, many go through periods of severe loneliness and may turn to drugs, alcohol, or attempt suicide for a way out. Many were born into family situations that were physically, emotionally, spiritually, and psychically abusive. These indigos had to figure out how to balance and keep their inherent integrity levels while being subjected to painful and life-shattering experiences. A large percentage was implanted in such horrendous situations as organized crime, physical abuse, sexual abuse, and mind control. Stress, Anxiety, addictions, fears, emotions, ADD, crystal, indigo bulimia, bipolar, etc.

The cofounder of Citizens Commission on Human Rights (CCHR), Dr. Thomas Szasz, professor emeritus of Psychiatry at the state of New York, Syracuse, is challenging his own profession to alert the American public of the potential danger in giving psychiatric drugs that he calls poison, not a treatment. He also tells us that psychiatrics have for hundreds of years used diagnostic terms, in the history of psychiatry, to stigmatize and control people. That no behavior or misbehavior is a disease or can be a disease…so cannot be treated by drugs.

What is Merkaba (Merkabah):

Merkaba, also spelled Merkabah, is the divine light vehicle allegedly used by ascended masters to connect and reach those in tune with the higher realms. It is your energy field and all other systems arises from it. The Merkaba is an ascension vehicle. It is your chakras, aura, meridians, organs, mind-body. Consciously attuning and activating it brings positive major life changes. Our bodies are holographic bodies of light. The Merkaba is alive. It is a living field, not a purely mechanical field of energy. Because it is a living field, it responds to human thought and feeling, which is the way to connect to the field. So the computer that guides the Merkaba is the human mind and heart. And the possibilities are endless.

Through the true living of qualities such as love, faith, trust, truth, and compassion, the Merkaba can spontaneously become alive. Very pure human character can translate into a living Merkaba field around the person and even if that person doesn't initially know it is there.

At certain and specific moment (not necessarily in this lifetime), a person's Merkaba field can become alive. When this happens, an electromagnetic change occurs, which results in a disc of energy that comes out from a tiny place near the base of the spine and quickly expands to about twenty-seven to thirty feet in radius around the body.

This disc can easily be perceived by scientific means, and if the United States Air Force is correct, it can be put up on their computer screens via satellite. In other words, the military can see people who activate their Merkabas and watch as they move around the surface of the earth.

Since the number of people who have done this is now in the millions, it is a fairly common sight now. It is the enormous magnetic burst that results from the disc expanding that brings attention to itself. This can easily be made invisible by people who activate their Merkabas, if they so desire.

The knowledge of the Merkaba is well-known by most of the more powerful governments of the world.

Mother Earth, the human race, and we as individuals can profit from this understanding and knowledge. The remembering of the Merkaba is unfolding all over the world, and it is all part of the evolving cosmic DNA. The Merkaba is a doorway or a dimensional window into a higher level of consciousness that is the catalyst for this great change called ascension.

ASCENSION OR THE END OF A CYCLE AND THE SHIFT OF THE ENERGY ASCENSION: THE DOOR TO THE DIVINE

Sacred mantra meditation—It is a form of prayer. The purpose of spiritual practice is to consciously connect with the soul (you). It is a state where we stay centered, and we quiet our mind to enable us to receive information. This gift offers clarity, expansion, and connection with your authentic expression as light. Even though you yearn for ascensions, you are surrounded by dense consciousness. It is often done by repetition of a word or by chanting a specific tone, like the one being done by Tibetan monks.

Tibetan monks in nirvanic harmony

Sounds/Biosound are notes that are colors that are wavelength and frequency. And what are we?

Sound healing offers profound results, which can be subtle and/ or instantaneous for those ready to receive healing.

When blocks are removed, your whole being returns to balance and better health is restored. Unconscious patterns of living manifest in your life as physical, mental, and emotional symptoms and pains. Your core beliefs, genetics, history, and soul wounds are the cause of discomfort and disease and are actually running your life.

As with nature, we are meant to live in perfect balance and vitality. When this is achieved, there are no pains, aches, discomforts, or disease. Sound healing clears whatever is stopping the life force from flowing and creates optimum health throughout our bodies. It assists us in accepting and experiencing higher levels of pain-free living.

Sound waves can amplify the effects upon acupressure points to relax muscles, increase circulation, and even reduce inflammation just by holding a transducer a few inches from the body and moving it slowly across the body's meridian, where acupressure points are located.

Ultrasound was looked at because it is useful in medicinal arenas for breaking up kidney stones and are cheaper to generate and direct.

Musicotherapy is a form of art therapy. Chinese found out that each internal organ has its own rhythm and by consequences vibrates to its own sound. These different internal organs correspond to these followings rhythm and by consequence vibrate sounds: Chui, Hu, Xi, Ke, Xu, and Xia.

And biosound healing provides a way of achieving prime health by eliminating blocks which keep us in patterns of self-sabotage and ways of holding ourselves back from living our full potential and joy.

Biosound healing also respects all belief system and honors all cultures and religion. It is Creator of all that is.

Sound and Music

For centuries, music and sound have been used for *healing* and transformation. From the guttural chanting of ancient shamans to the Gregorian chants of the cathedrals, sound and music have played a central role in the culture of humanity. Only recently we have begun to understand the psychological effects of sound and music on the brain. We know that music can play a crucial role on the brain. The vibratory nature of sound and music creates a language that the body and mind understand.

Music also has a profound impact on emotional problems and learning difficulties, as shown by the work of Dr. Tomatis in France. It is quite interesting how Dr. Tomatis got involved in his work with sound therapy. Somewhat early in his studies, he was called to a Benedictine monastery outside of Paris. The monks were depressed and were having trouble eating and sleeping. Dr. Tomatis was asked to find the cause of their ailments. In the course of his explorations, he discovered that the abbey had recently acquired a new abbot. The new father prided himself on being a modern man, and considering the Gregorian chants too medieval, he ordered the monks to stop chanting.

Without knowing it, the abbot had taken away a primary form of brain stimulation for the monks. When Dr. Tomatis had the abbot reinstate the chanting, the depression lifted, and the monks were fine. This incident led D. Tomatis to study the effects of sound on the brain. In the course of his work, he discovered the effects of high frequencies on brain processing, emotional problems, and block learning.

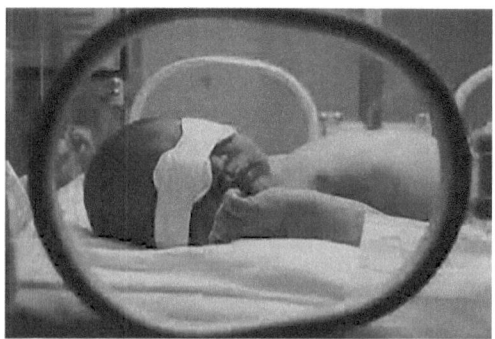

Chromotherapy (light therapy), sound
(biosound), music therapy (art therapy)

Color Harmonics, the Healing Colors, and Their Use and Adjusting the Body's Oscillations by Sound

Sounds are nirvanic harmony and this is what the Tibetan monks are doing.

All body cells have membrane-like characteristics that are capable of acting as sound receivers. Our bodies are living bio-oscillators, as are all living systems, and are similar to crystal receiving sets (as in every radio and TV set) in that they can absorb vibrations of sound (audible or not). A series of billions upon billions of vibrating atomic particles that make up our cells resonate to incoming sound vibrations.

Each parts of the body (cells, tissues, organs) has its own frequency response. Most of the vibratory effects occur below our conscious awareness.

- *Do*—is red and hydrogen; stimulate the liver, heart, prostate, teeth, lymphatic system
- *Re*—is orange and calcium, selenium, copper; good for depression, emotion in movement, brings joy
- *Mi*—is yellow and magnesium, carbon, sodium; good for concentration, stomach, and skin
- *Fa*—is green and chlorine, barium; a nurturing color; lungs, heart, blood pressure, weight loss, and cellulite
- *So*—is cyan blue and oxygen, indium; very calming; for throat, neck, arm
- *La*—is indigo blue and bismuth, ionium; peace and calming
- *Ti*—is violet and cobalt, actinium; perfect color for meditation

Colorology is an alternative medicine method and chromotherapists use color and light to balance energy wherever a person's body be lacking, be it physical, emotional, spiritual, or mental. Color, or colour, is the visual, perceptual property corresponding in humans to the categories called red, yellow, blue, and others. Color derives from the spectrum of light (distribution of light energy versus wave-length) interacting in the eye with the spectral sensitivities of the light receptors. Color categories and physical specifications of color are also associated with objects, materials, light sources, etc., based on their physical properties such as light absorption, reflection, or emission spectra.

The science of color is sometimes called chromatics. It includes the perception of color by the human eye and brain, the origin of color in materials, color theory in art, and the physics of electromagnetic radiation in the visible range (that is, what we commonly refer to simply as light).

Color harmonics frequency and geometric forms, crystalline mineral-based color, and geometric light is applied to specific areas and acupoints on the body. It is acupuncture without needle. Colors get also associated with both positive and negative effects in color therapy, specific colors and accurate amounts of color are deemed to be critical in healing. Therapeutic color is often combined with aromatherapy, pure therapeutic grade of essential oils, in an attempt to heighten the therapeutic effect.

Full-spectrum light travels from the eye to the brain, where it triggers the hypothalamus to send chemical messengers to regulate the autonomic functions of the body, such as blood pressure, breathing, digestion, and the immune system, as well as the body's circadian rhythm. In order to maintain health, it may be important to be exposed to light containing the full wavelength spectrum found in natural light. Full-spectrum light therapy, bright light therapy, and ultraviolet light therapy are used by some clinicians for treating conditions that range from seasonal affective disorder to bulimia, and new applications are continually being suggested.

In its usage, which can be assimilated to the Chinese traditional medicine, the benefit changes and depends on the colors applied. Each chakras, meridians, and associated organs corresponds also to a specific color.

When we are in a state of loving, we get smooth brainwaves. Those brainwaves in turn strengthen the spin field in gravity and the earth is made *healthy*.

When we are in a state of chaos, our brainwaves get very violent. This affects the spin of gravity and creates stress in the earth.

When enough people create static and chaos, it creates a pressure buildup in the surrounding area and we have in return earthquakes, volcanoes, and natural disasters as a result. But the negative forces have little time left, and we can and need to stop them.

On other planets, the composition of the air is not so different except that the air is purer and the luminosity is much superior and there is also less gravity. The vibration is different and there is no disease.

Before anything, before the big bang was a *Spirit. God* the Creator is Spirit. The illusionary world came into creation when the consciousness of the created split from our Creator's consciousness. And it is when we forgot the oneness and when we began to believe that we were separated from God. The Source/God/Creator wanted to experience life and feelings in a physical body, but he wanted only to experience good thoughts. But out of distortion evolved the ego, and we created the polarity of sickness and health, life and death, love and fear, war and peace, and sorrow and joy. Each being has been created from God. We are souls/multidimensional bodies/astral bodies (and if we astral project ourselves for more than seventy-two hours, the body goes to its higher-self because it is the universal law, our cross over, and stay there—coma).

We all chose our parents before coming to earth. We are multi-dimensional beings/soul entity choosing a physical body to incarnate. We make a contract with our higher self (it is a part of ourselves) before being born. Our higher self knows the exact date and time of our death.

That is why suicide should not even be considered because your higher self is your guardian angel. It shows you the video of your life and then erases everything. By free will you can kill yourself, but you will reincarnate within forty-nine days. You never want to do that because your higher self makes sure that you finish your contract and you will reincarnate within the forty-nine days that follow your suicide.

We were all subconsciously programmed to die when we separated ourselves from our Creator. And because of this, even the happiest of humans are to die *if* they stay trapped in an "illusion with feelings" that they are unworthy to live and believe that life is too much of a struggle, guilt—they will activate, then, the death hormone. Aligning our mind to the mind of God (the Creator, the Source) is the only way to free us from death because it is within His consciousness that eternal life exists. Religion has programmed humans for death and heaven (or hell). Once people get there, once people will align themselves to the mind of the Creator, it will follow a shift in consciousness. It will be the end of earth's destruction (environment). There will be the release of new technologies available. Peace will prevail in the world, and it will be the end of poverty. Shortly after the announcement of the new technologies, it will follow a new financial system.

Our higher self is omnipotent and omnipresent. Your intuition comes from your higher self helping you. Your higher self is your teacher and can make anything. It can make miracles. Guides are different; they are nice entities helping us during our experience on that planet. They have no faces, only vague forms.

If you have any question to which you need answer, you must ask your higher self. We have long forgotten the abilities that the consciousness of the physical body carries, and your body is also connected to your divine blueprint.

But we can communicate with it. We can ask it questions and it will answer.

Meditate and ask to make contact. Put your hands in pray pose first. There is a purpose, and the church has forgotten why, but there is a purpose to it. You can call for healing, answers, and help:

1. Begin by focusing at the heart center.
2. Believe that you already know the solution.
3. Continue focusing on your heart center and ask to be shown the answer.
4. The first idea that comes into your head is the answer. Image, symbol, or thought, it's the first one.

Bach Flower Remedies are a complete system of thirty-eight remedies that help us rediscover the positive side of ourselves. Everyone is different, and for emotional eating support you may find you need some different or additional flower remedies.

For example, Walnut helps to protect you from change you may be experiencing in your life. Rock Water helps when you push yourself too hard trying to set a good example.

Or if you hide your troubles behind a smile, try Agrimony.

So whether you need support to stay positive about maintaining good eating habits or lack a positive self-image, look for Bach Flower Remedies for help.

Bach Flower Remedies

In the 1920s and '30s, a noted homeopath, Dr. Edward Bach, discovered a system of flower remedies that can help us rediscover the positive side of ourselves. He believed, as many doctors do today, that attitude of mind plays a vital role in maintaining health and recovering from illness. When he died in 1936, he had developed a complete system of thirty-eight flower remedies, each prepared from the flowers of wild plants, trees, and bushes. The remedies work by treating the individual rather than the disease or its symptoms. Still made in the UK at Mount Vernon, the home of Dr. Bach, *Bach® Original Flower Remedies* are the only flower remedies bearing Edward Bach's signature on each bottle.

Today, these gentle remedies are used worldwide and are sold in over sixty-six countries.

> Nothing in nature can hurt us when we are happy and in harmony; on the contrary, all nature is there for our use and our enjoyment.
>
> —*Dr. Edward Bach*

Bach Flower Remedies are a complete system of thirty-eight remedies that help us rediscover the positive side of ourselves. Everyone is different, and for emotional eating support, you may find you need some different or additional flower remedies.

For example, Walnut helps to protect you from change you may be experiencing in your life. Rock Water helps when you push yourself too hard trying to set a good example. Or if you hide your troubles behind a smile, try Agrimony.

So whether you need support to stay positive about maintaining good eating habits or lack a positive self-image, look for Bach Flower Remedies for help.

THERAPEUTIC ESSENTIAL OILS (AROMATHERAPY) THE IMPORTANCE OF FREQUENCY OF ESSENTIAL OILS

According to Ancient Egyptian hieroglyphics and Chinese manuscripts, priests and physicians were using essential oils thousands of years before Christ to heal the sick. They are the oldest form of medicine and cosmetic known to man and were considered more valuable than gold. There are hundreds of references to oils in the Bible. The wise men brought the Christ Child gold, frankincense, and myrrh. (Clinical research now shows that frankincense oil contains very high immune stimulating properties.) Some of the precious oils that have been used since antiquity for anointing and healing the sick are frankincense, myrrh, galbanum, hyssop, cassia, cinnamon, and spikenard. Science is only now beginning to investigate the incredible healing substances found in essential oils. With their immune stimulating properties, EO dramatically enhance and support the building of the immune system, whether there are inhaled or rubbed on the body topically.

The effectiveness of essential oils cannot be fully understood without some discussion of frequency. Frequency is the measurable rate of electrical energy flow that is constant between any two points. Everything has frequency. Pure Essential Oils have very high frequency. Dr. Robert O. Becker, in his book *The Body* Electric, establishes that the human body has an electrical frequency and that much about a person's health can be determined by one's frequency.

In 1992, Bruce Tainio of Tainio Technology, an independent division of Eastern State University in Cheney, Washington, built the first frequency monitor in the world. Tainio has determined that the average frequency of the human body during the day time is 62–68 Hz. (A healthy body frequency is 62–72 Hz.)

When the frequency drops, the immune system is compromised. If the frequency drops to 58 Hz, cold and flu symptoms appear. At 55 Hz, diseases like candida take hold; at 52 Hz, Epstein-Barr; and at 42 Hz, cancer.

According to Dr. Royal Rife, every disease has a frequency. He found that certain frequencies can prevent the development of disease and that others would destroy disease. Substances with higher frequency will destroy diseases of lower frequency.

The study of frequencies raises an important question concerning the frequencies of substances we eat, breath, and absorb.

Many pollutants lower healthy frequency:

- Dry herbs from 12 to 22 Hz and fresh herbs from 20 to 27 Hz
- Processed/canned food has a frequency of zero.
- Fresh produce has up to 15 Hz
- Essential oils start at 52 Hz and go as high as 320 Hz, the frequency of Pure Rose Oil.

Clinical research shows that essential oils have the highest frequency of any natural substance known to man creating an environment in which disease, bacteria, virus, fungus, etc., cannot live. Theories are yesterday's wisdom, tomorrow's destiny.

Essential oils are the oldest and some of the most powerful therapeutic agents known. They have enjoyed a millennium-long history of use in healing and anointing throughout the ancient world. Frankincense to cure every ailment from gout to a broken head. Myrrh, lotus, and sandalwood oils were widely used in Ancient Egyptian purification and embalming rituals. Essential oils are some of the most concentrated natural extracts known, exerting significant antiviral, anti-inflammatory, antibacterial, hormonal, and psychological effects. Essential oils have the ability to penetrate cell membranes, travel throughout the blood and tissues, and enhance electrical frequencies.

After using them, there is no doubt that essential oils were ordained as the medicine for mankind and will be held as the medicine of our future: the missing link of modern medicine where allopathic and holistic medicine joins together for the leap into the twenty-first century.

Essential oils to use for prevention or to eliminate flus, colds, and sickness if you do happen to catch something, apply on spine, bottom of feet, or diffuse in the air:

- lemon
- Thieves—don't forget the Thieves Cough Drops
- drops, spray, and hand cleaner
- hyssop
- Exodus II
- ImmunPower

For respiratory, apply over lungs, back, top of feet, diffuse, or place in a pan of hot water and inhale steam:

- Dorado Azul
- eucalyptus
- Raven
- RC

You can add some "vitality oils" to your family's smoothies and food to get the many benefits of assisting digestion, adding flavor, as well as building up the immune system. When adding to hot soups/ drinks, make sure to add the oil after it has cooled down. This will prevent destroying the therapeutic properties of the oils.

Benefit of Inhaling and Reducing Pollution by Using Essential Oils

Several studies have found that it reduces airborne bacteria, and that also attendance in schools increased as it reduces the presence of numerous pollutants. It is also very helpful for asthmatic people and keeps home mold free.

Ultrasonic diffusers—uses frequency vibrations to convert essential oils and water into billowing clouds and fragrant, therapeutic vapor. You are constantly surrounded by fragrance and a soothing and purifying mist.

Nebulizer diffusers—they range from simple evaporative devices to sophisticated nebulizers that infuse the air with microscopic droplets of pure essential oils.

*One of the Most Important Young Living Kit
The Feelings Kit from Young Living Pure
and Therapeutic Essential Oils*

Valor

Put Valor oil on the soles of both feet at nighttime along with Highest Potential blend. These blends are effective to erase limited thinking. Valor balances and equalizes the body's energies, thereby increasing oxygen intake to the pineal gland—the seat of our higher intelligence and intuitive faculties. You will wake up in the morning more self-assured and more alive to start the day.

Harmony

Massage one drop of Harmony oil on each of the energy center points of your body. There are seven of them along the spine: coccyx, sacrum, lumbar, dorsal (heart), cervical (where neck meets shoulders), medulla (hollow place at center base of skull), and pineal (center of forehead). You can also massage Harmony on the crown of the head.

Harmony balances the parasympathetic and sympathetic nervous systems, which in turn gives us progressive creativity and feelings of confidence. "The biggest sin is not having confidence in you," says Gary Young. "He who lacks confidence lacks life."

Forgiveness

Apply Forgiveness oil around the navel with the right hand going clockwise several times and think of situations where you need to forgive yourself or others. We beat up on ourselves, but everyone makes mistakes. Yet we struggle to forgive our own mistakes and those of others. Unable to forgive is one of the most common roots of physical, mental, and spiritual disease. Unforgiveness does not make the offending party sick; it makes us sick. Forgiveness is for our own benefit. It is accomplished in five steps: 1) Forgive yourself for allowing the person to affect your health and happiness. 2) Forgive the other person for any harm he or she may have caused you. (This need not be done directly with the person being forgiven but is an inner adjustment on your part.) 3) Give the other person permission to forgive you. 4) See the good in the situation. 5) Be thankful for the experience and the lesson it taught you. Inhale and apply Forgiveness oil while going through these steps and repeat as often as necessary to clear the feelings of unforgiveness.

All must be forgiven but it does not mean that all must be forgotten. The old grudge is to bottle up the poison and toxicity, so you must forgive. Psychological problems could be from unforgiveness. But be aware! Do not *ever* get trap in this matrix with drugs.

Release

Negative energy goes into the blood and then into the liver for cleansing where the toxins can remain trapped. Thus the liver becomes a storage place for anger, resentment, bitterness, hatred, jealousy, envy, addictions, and a host of destructive feelings. Apply a few drops of Release oil on your tongue to release the poisons of stored emotions from the liver. Rub Release over the liver area. Drink lots of pure water and do a liver cleanse.

Present Time

When we live in the past or dwell on the future, we are not being productive in the present. Energize three drops of Present Time by making clockwise circles of the oil on the palm of your hand, and then apply it to your thymus (the gland just under your sternum or breastbone). Besides keeping you focused on the tasks of today, this can also help you financially by increasing your abundance consciousness in the present.

Inner Child

"When you are a child all things are possible. There are no limitations," says Gary Young. "When you find your inner child, you have found your true self. The child in you is your creativity." Apply one drop of Inner Child onto the pad of your thumb and then place your thumb onto the roof of your mouth. This opens the cranial sutures and stimulates the pineal, pituitary, and other organs of the emotional brain that occupy the space just above the roof of your mouth. Walking backward while you have your thumb in your mouth looks stupid, but it changes the rotation in the pelvis, elongating the spine, and decompressing the discs in your back. Thus, you can clear the nerve channels for energy to flow smoothly throughout your brain and body.

Then you have the emergency kit (everything you need to travel) called the Essential Seven™. It contains seven oils and oil blends:

- *Lavender*—calming and relaxing. It will calm you and help you sleep and is the first aid in case of a burn.

- *Lemon*—put a few drops in your water. Cleansing properties for air, water, and is supportive to a normal immune system (Vitamin C).
- *Peppermint*—normalize digestive system, will give you energy, helps restore mental alertness or wakefulness from fatigue or drowsiness
- *Joy*—It inspires feelings of romance and togetherness and will lift you up.
- *Pan Away*—relief of muscle and joint discomfort.
- *Peace and Calming*—promotes deep sense of peace and is ideal to calm children.
- *Purification*—to cleanse skin, the interior home surfaces, on airplanes, hotel room, or offices.

The Supreme Science Qigong That became Press on Chi (Energy)

We believe that the power of these Qigong healing techniques can transform the world. The life force is all around us. A veritable "sea of Qi." Transmitting Qi and healing is the art of transferring vital energy to another human being.

Do You Have to Be a Vegetarian to Raise Your Consciousness? No.

Stop eating and start nourishing. Begin by replacing the word *eating* by *nourishing*. From there, your awareness and your food choice will naturally shift. You must do the following:

- Listen to your body, eat more often and smaller proportions.
- Bless your food (it brings your energy and help you digest) and your drinks for thirty seconds.
- Drink a lot of pure water.

- Watch your pH.
- Learn to rest well. Listen to your body again.
- Meditate for twenty minutes every day, and exercise at least walk twenty minutes for two to three times a week, but five times is the best.

"Enlightenment, or to be In-Light, is a state of being that exists with tangible availability than ever before for those who choose to embrace it."

"Time is folding in upon itself as the energies on the planet rapidly escalate; your third-dimensional experience is *shifting!*"

"When we finally stop cutting deals with the Divine, the gifts that we receive are endless. This is one such gift."

ANGEL IS AN ASCENDED NONMATTER GLORIOUSLY EXPRESSING LIGHT AND LOVE

Our work, CHADD and VIE, is our gift to share with you. We are offering you a process designed to reconnect you to your original fullness with the universe and God.

It is about awakening your light body in personalized sessions to remove any energy blockages. And you will, thereafter, stop resisting your growth to move out of stuck places.

We use sound frequency, spectra-light (chroma light), geometrical forms, and the Divine energy according to the individual needs of the client. Our work clears and raises one's vibrational levels to restores your intimate connection to the Divine self and allows the activation of all DNA strands, in which the name of God is encrypted.

To heal, you must retune the incorrect vibrations at the levels of cause and symptoms and also have your vibration raised.

The use of the spectra-light "crystalline" color lenses (not in tinted glass, not in plastic, not gel) applied to meridians (acupuncture points) and combined to sacred geometric forms to achieve the healing through the reconnection of the ax atonal lines with specific sound frequency, then the Divine Father (the Source) calls before him the unity that has been perfectly balanced between the bodies.

Some neurological changes happen in the body while we raise your vibrations. The complete body is transformed. The two parts of the brain once separated are reconnected. Blocks and emotions are released for the evolution of your soul. The reconnection brings in new axiatonal lines.

Divine reconnection removes the energetic blockages allowing embodiment of your higher self, the part of you closest to Source, or God. Expansion of your consciousness is one of the main benefits; you will simply become more aware, especially of what your purpose is and why you incarnated here at this point in time. Your dormant brain functions will start to become active, especially your pineal gland. Some of the physical benefits reported by clients include increased energy and clarity of thoughts. You will start to see how your body is just a thought form, and you can change your body more easily with focus. Your body will undergo a detoxification, which will bring old emotional issues to the surface to be released forever that will no longer cause disease and poison the body. There are certain blockages that everyone has that prevent DNA from naturally activating.

We always give an auric clearing and a karmic session *first*. Once you are free from these blockages, then we can activate your DNA.

The basic process is about five sessions minimum. It begins with an auric clearing (your aura). The auric clearing must be done first to remove all of the highest priority energetic blockages. About a week later, after your light body becomes stabilized in its new energetic structure, the karmic session can be done. This session removes past life karmic issues that are keeping you in a "loop," where the same types of things keep happening to you over and over in life. The following sessions prepare you to accumulate more light and energy required to activate your DNA. About a week after the karmic session, the first DNA activation can be done. There are at least four to twelve DNA activations required to activate as many strands of DNA that your energy body can handle at this point in your evolution, and the sessions should be done about a week apart. These sessions promote permanent, lifelong changes and are given with a gentle, loving intent.

The language of light is cosmic light intelligence carried in color streams of consciousness, a place where everything is possible.

As the world consciousness rises in vibration and in awareness, you must do all that you can on a personal level to join in this transformation. Prepare yourself. Choose the spiritual path. Peace of mind is not just a little gift. You can achieve peace and joy. You have a chance of finding your way through the veils of forgetfulness, back to where you came and belong. Your resurrection is in your reawakening.

TAKE CONTROL OF YOUR OWN HEALTH! (GET THOSE CHEMICALS OUT OF YOUR LIFE)

• •

Essential oils are energy molecules alive; drugs are not. We are distributors of Young Living Essential Oils, and we would like to share with you this fabulous products from this company and 101 uses for the Young Living® Thieves® products.

Welcome to the Wonderful World of Thieves®

Thieves® Oil Blend is formulated with highly antiviral, antiseptic, antibacterial, and anti-infectious essential oils. Thieves® Oil Blend was created based on research of a group of fifteenth century thieves in France who protected themselves by rubbing themselves with cloves, rosemary, and other aromatics while robbing plague victims. This Young Living proprietary blend was university tested and found to be highly effective in supporting the immune system and good health. This proprietary blend has also been documented to kill over 99.96 percent of bacteria it comes into contact with.

Thieves® Oil Blend—use directly from bottle, diffuse, or dilute with purified water to spritz. We strongly recommend you to buy a nebulizer. All others method will burn the live molecules.

Ingredients

- *Clove (Syzygium aromaticum)* has a sweet, spicy fragrance that is stimulating and revitalizing. An important ingredient in Thieves® Blend due to its wonderful immune-enhancing features, its principal constituent is eugenol, an element that is used in the dental industry to numb gums. Clove is the highest-scoring single ingredient ever tested for its antioxidant capacity on the ORAC scale.
- *Lemon (Citrus limón)* has antiseptic-like properties and contains compounds that amplify immunity. It promotes circulation, leukocyte formation, and lymphatic function.
- *Cinnamon Bark (Cinnamomum verum)* has the wonderful cinnamon scent loved around the world. Warming and stimulating, it is comforting during the cold season. Many people find it highly romantic. Historically, cinnamon was so popular, it was the main reason behind the occupation of Ceylon by first the Portuguese, then the Dutch and then the British.
- *Eucalyptus (Eucalyptus radiata)* is cooling, refreshing, and energizing. Lighter in smell than Eucalyptus globulus, it nevertheless has many of the same health-supporting properties. Because it is relatively gentle and non-irritating, it is the preferred choice for children. This variety is one of the most versatile of the eucalyptus oils and is suitable for topical use, diffusing, and even direct inhalation. It

has long been an ingredient in some of our most popular blends.
- *Rosemary (Rosmarinus officinalis ct cineol)* has a fresh, herbaceous, sweet, slightly medicinal aroma. Energizing oil, it may be beneficial for helping to restore mental alertness when experiencing fatigue.

Caution: Do not use on children under four years of age. It is also a popular ingredient in skin and hair care products.

Thieves Cleaner Essential Oil Proportion Guide

Note: One capful of Thieves Cleaner = ½ tablespoon

- *Light Degreasing*—1 capful Thieves Cleaner to 3¾ cups of water
- *Medium Degreasing*—1 capful Thieves Cleaner to a little less than 2 cups of water
- *Heavy Degreasing*—1 capful cleaner to a little less than 1 cup of water
- *Hand Cleaner*—½ cup thieves cleaner to ½ cup water
- *Dishwasher*—1 capful of Thieves Cleaner
- *Pots and Pans*—½ capful of Thieves Cleaner to 3+ cups of water
- *Floors*—1 capful of Thieves Cleaner to 6¼ cups of water
- *Walls*—1 capful of Thieves Cleaner to a little less than 2 cups of water
- *Fabrics, Carpet Spotting, etc.*—1 capful of Thieves Cleaner to 2 cups of water
- *Washing Machine (Laundry)*—Depending on size of washer, use 1 to 2 capfuls of Thieves Cleaner
- *Carpet*—1 capful of thieves cleaner to 6¼ cups of water
- *Glass/Windows*—1 capful of Thieves Cleaner to 5 quarts of water

Use this fantastic cleaner to clean your sinks, toilets, showers, etc. Giving it a great smell instead of that awful chemical smell from using other store-bought stuff. It also works great in cleaning the outside of the greasy barbeque grill and stand. We have even used it to spray on bugs, and it works.

Anti means "against." *Microbial* is a minute living organism, minute forms of life capable of causing disease including bacteria and fungi.

Essential oils create an unfriendly environment, which becomes deadly to disease-causing bacteria, viruses, and other pathogens.

Favorite Uses for Thieves® Antimicrobial Blend of Essential Oils

1. Dilute with V-6™ Enhanced Vegetable Oil Complex and apply to cuts or open wounds to prevent infection and promote healing.
2. Mix with a tablespoon of water, gargle, and swallow for a sore throat.
3. Apply it undiluted, directly to the skin of your upper chest and throat for bronchitis.
4. Place a drop on your thumb and apply to the roof of your mouth for a headache.
5. Put 10–12 drops in a size 00 capsule undiluted and swallow daily for longevity.
6. For acne, take internally and apply to the skin diluted with Young Living's V-6™ carrier oil.
7. Put directly on the soles of your feet to protect you from colds and flu.
8. Breathe in the vapors when you have lung congestion.
9. Use to clean pet cages, creating a healthier environment for them.
10. Add to your dishwasher for cleaner dishes.
11. Add to your laundry cycle for cleaner clothes.

12. Add to your mop water for cleaner floors.
13. Mix with water to make a spray to repel insects on your flowers and plants.
14. Use to dissolve the gummy adhesive on price labels.
15. Apply to bee and wasp stings to neutralize the toxin and relieve the pain.
16. Apply to gums to prevent and treat gum disease.
17. Apply orally to maintain healthy teeth and reduce cavities.
18. Apply to gums and teeth for pain relief from toothaches.
19. Diffuse in homes or business to solve mold problems.
20. Add to orange juice and drink to reduce phlegm and congestion.
21. Apply to broken bones or joints for pain relief and to hasten healing.
22. Put a drop in your cup of tea for flavor and to maintain health.
23. Put on the tip of your tongue to help you stop smoking.
24. Put on cold sores and canker sores to make them disappear.
25. For warts, apply topically, inhale, and ingest in capsules to make them disappear.
26. Rub on sore joints to relieve arthritis pain.
27. Drink a few drops in water or juice every three hours to stop a cold.
28. Place a drop on the tongue and a drop in a glass of water every day for herpes.
29. Rub on the bottom of children's feet for protection before school every day.
30. Diffuse in the house as your children come home from school every day to kill airborne bacteria.
31. Mix 50:50 with V-6™ vegetable oil and rub on daily for relief of shingles.
32. Apply a drop on wound of a cat or dog to enhance healing.
33. Diffuse in the home or office to stimulate a cheerful mood.

34. Diffuse in the office to increase concentration and work efficiency.
35. Diffuse in your place of business to ward off germs.
36. Diffuse in the classroom to reduce student sickness and absenteeism.
37. Put a few drops in your carpet steamer/cleaner to disinfect carpet.
38. Mix a few drops with honey or agave in a teaspoon for cough relief.
39. Breathe and apply for sinus headaches.
40. Put a drop on a pimple to make it shrink and disappear.
41. For laryngitis, put a drop under your tongue to restore your voice.
42. Inhale for relief of allergy symptoms.
43. Take a capsule full every day for relief of Lyme disease symptoms.
44. Carry an EO pendant on every flight to protect you from germs on the plane.
45. Drop in the heat/AC vents of a hotel to rid it of airborne germs.
46. Mix with baking soda to clean bathtubs.
47. Apply undiluted to the toes and feet to combat fungus.
48. Apply to poison ivy rashes (may need to be diluted with vegetable oil) to relieve the itch.
49. Drop Thieves® Oil Blend on a cloth to remove permanent marker stains.
50. Sanitize pierced earrings by cleaning with Thieves® Oil Blend.
51. Rub on the big toe before retiring to help with proper vision.
52. Applying Thieves® Oil Blend, diluted 1 drop oil to 5 drops V-6™ Mixing Oil, may be helpful in soothing pink eye and other eye inflammations. (Do not get in the eye.)

53. Apply 1 drop of Thieves® Oil Blend onto toothbrush to sanitize.

A Special Antibiotic Formula

In a double aught "00" capsule, combine 10–12 drops of Thieves® Essential Oil Blend with 6–8 drops of oregano, and 2 drops of frankincense.

Thieves® Household Cleaner Proportion Guide

- One capful of Thieves® Cleaner = 1 teaspoon.
- Best if used with purified water (do not use water that contains chlorine).
- The goal is a chemically free environment, living healthy naturally.

1. All-purpose Thieves® Cleaner in a spray bottle—1 capful Thieves® Cleaner to 1 quarts water
2. Light Degreasing—1 capful Thieves® Cleaner to 3¾ cups of water
3. Medium Degreasing—1 capful Thieves® Cleaner to 2 cups water
4. Heavy Degreasing—1 capful Thieves® Cleaner to 1 cup water
5. Window and glass cleaner—1 capful Thieves® Cleaner to 5 quarts water or ¼ teaspoon to a quart of water for spray bottles
6. Hand cleaner—½ cup Thieves® Cleaner to ½ cup water
7. Dishwasher—1 capful Thieves® Cleaner
8. Pot and Pans—½ capful of Thieves® Cleaner to 3 cups water
9. Floors—1 capful Thieves® Cleaner to 6¼ cups water

10. Walls—1 capful Thieves® Cleaner to a little less than 2 cups water
11. Fabrics—1 capful Thieves® Cleaner to 2 cups water
12. Laundry—Depending on size of washer, use 1 to 2 capfuls of Thieves® Cleaner
13. Carpet—1 capful Thieves® Cleaner to 6 ¼+ cups water

Thieves® Household Cleaner (Continued)

54. Use for bathrooms and toilets to sanitize and freshen.
55. Use to cut grease on kitchen counters and stovetops.
56. Use to mop floors to clean and disinfect.
57. Apply to hands to remove stubborn, sticky substances like tree sap.
58. Use to wash fruits and vegetables from the supermarket.
59. Add to the water in your vacuum cleaner/steamer to cleanse the air and disinfect the carpet.
60. Spray along ant trails in the house to keep them out.
61. Use to wipe chairs and furniture in school classrooms to cut down on student sickness.
62. Scrub old floors to remove old varnish and prepare for refinishing. (www.youngliving.com/helene398498)
63. Clean upholstery.
64. Clean the upholstery and dashboard of your car.
65. Soak off burnt food in pots and skillets.
66. Wipe or soak garbage cans to get them clean, sanitary, and smelling fresh.
67. For tough stains, pour it on as a prewash stain remover.
68. Use undiluted to clean and kill mold on walls and floors or degrease oven.

Mold Solution

Diffuse the Thieves® Oil Blend continuously for twenty-four hours in the room containing mold. Determining the length of diffusion time is directly related to the severity of mold.

Clean visible mold with Thieves® Household Cleaner. To prevent mold,

1. Diffuse Thieves® essential oil.
2. Eliminate leaks and moisture.
3. Clean thoroughly using Thieves® Household Cleaner.

Uses for Antimicrobial Thieves® Lozenges

69. Take with the first sniffle and signs of a cold or sore throat to ward it off.
70. Take prior to singing performances to keep the voice strong and hit the high notes.
71. Use to hasten the healing when a cold or flu has been contracted.
72. Suck on one as you enter an airplane to protect you from germs onboard.

Uses for Antimicrobial Thieves® Mouthwash

73. Rinse daily for clean breath and to keep teeth and gums healthy.
74. Gargle before a singing engagement to clear mucus.

Uses for Thieves® Waterless Hand Purifier

75. Use as a healthy alternative to soap and water to sanitize hands.

76. Rub on hands to make them soft, fresh, and smooth.
77. Apply to face to clear acne.

Uses for Antimicrobial Thieves® Bar Soap

78. Rub on stains as a prewash stain remover.
79. Use as a deodorant or antibacterial hand soap.

Uses for Antimicrobial Thieves® Spray

80. Spray on doorknobs in public restrooms to kill germs.
81. Spray in the throat to restore a lost voice.
82. Spray hands before and after shaking hands with a lot of people.
83. Spray in restrooms on airplanes to reduce airborne bacteria.
84. Spray on vegetables and fruits when washing them.
85. Carry for protection in countries with cholera, malaria, or dysentery.
86. Use as an air freshener for cooking odors or other unwanted smells.
87. Take to the gym and spray all the equipment you use.
88. Take to the supermarket and use to disinfect shopping cart handles.
89. Use in the classroom for desks, tables, and other items handled by children.
90. Spray in your mouth and throat at first onset of cold or bronchitis.
91. Spray on shower stalls and bathroom walls to kill and remove mold.

Uses for Antimicrobial Thieves® Toothpaste

92. Brush every day to prevent cavities and gum disease.
93. Use when teeth have been damaged or broken to help them heal.

94. Use to prevent or heal gum disease.
95. Apply as an underarm deodorant.

Uses for Antimicrobial Thieves® Wipes

96. Wipe doorknobs and other things touched by the public.
97. Wipe dirty piano keys to clean and disinfect.
98. Use to clean children's hands when traveling.
99. Use on the steering wheel and gearshift of your vehicle.
100. Use on public telephones to remove germs.
101. Use on public computer keyboards and mice.

Obligatory disclaimer: The information in this book is intended for educational purposes only. These statements have not been evaluated by the Food and Drug Administration. These products are not intended to diagnose, treat, cure, or prevent any disease. Anyone suffering from any disease, illness, or injury should consult with a physician.

All suggested uses apply only to the use of therapeutic grade Young Living™ essential oils.

> If you want to understand the Secrets of the Universe, think of energy, frequency and vibration.
>
> —Nikola Tesla

The notion of clean, inexpensive energy for everyone, however, is a threat to those who want to soak every last dollar out of fossil fuels and especially those who would use control of energy to dictate people's lives.

Shortly before his death in 1943, Tesla had submitted a proposal to FDR to counter the damaging potential of fission-based nuclear energy development. He claimed in his proposal to the president that he knew of a method by which we could get all of the energy we could ever use from the space that surrounds us.

The meeting that was scheduled with FDR as a result of this proposal never occurred. Tesla was found dead in his New York apartment. The official report attributed his death to natural causes but many were not satisfied that this was the case.

—Adam Trombly

Light and sound are the medicine of the future.

—Edgar Cayce

All humans are holographic bodies of light and in a tetrahedron. We are light, we are colors (your aura is and each of your organs are also of different colors) and energy (chakras are vortex of energy); we are also wavelength and frequency.

Sound and light resonant vibration change the human brain and body. Harmonic frequencies rapidly rebalance the natural energy of your body and mind. Sound waves amplify the effects upon acupuncture points and relax muscles, increase circulation, and reduce inflammation. Light works on cellular, immune, and on all levels. Now every disease, or unease, in the body start in your aura, and if you keep your body stressed too long at one point, it turns into symptoms.

Every symptom is emotion(s) trapped in your body. Like anger is trapped in your liver, and this is one of the reason you are asked most of the time to begin by cleansing your liver by all natural or holistic therapists. Once the first step is achieved, you'll be able to clear your stuck emotions from your past (from your previous lives), and your body will be rebalanced to accrete the amount of light, raise your vibrations to finally activate the necessary strands of DNA from which you have all been cut from since the fall of Atlantis. The two parts of your brain that was once separated will be reconnected then.

Light is also sound, and it is also wavelength and frequency and as VIE works with spectra-light and sacred geometric forms, tetrahedron, cube, flower of life, and much more advanced forms (the choice will all depend on what your body will need at that moment), CHADD, the sound expert, work with specific sound/biosound during office sessions. It heals emotions, cells, DNA, blood, and immune system during the light energy sessions. It takes usually between three to five sessions.

And when most people think about healing, they focus on the notion of someone suffering from an ailment or injury who gets better. But what does it mean to *get better?*

Better than what? Better than they were at some moment in their past? Better than someone else is? Getting better is far too limiting a definition of healing. Thinking in that way divests us of our birth right to be in direct communion with God/love/the universe and therefore to be self-sustaining, self-healing beings. Healing, as we often tend to think of it, may well be about the alleviation of symptoms, diseases, infirmities, and other noticeable hindrances to full functioning. But healing is also the restoration of the person to spiritual wholeness. In essence, healing is the release or removal of a block or interference that has kept us separate from the perfection of the universe. Yet healing is about our evolution and also includes the evolutionary restructuring of our DNA and our reconnection to the universe on a new level.

The genetic composition of the body is changing. It is preparing us for the uplift in consciousness.

Energy is quickening and dark forces try to weaken people's mind bodies, tiring them out like frozen or locked up energies, like a chronic fatigue condition, and turning people away from the pure sharpness and clarity of their mind. Right now opposite forces are out to stop all spiritually aware people and even like workers. And there will be many who will not withstand the change of energy pattern from the past; they will perish during the three-day period. It is just that the physical body will not be able to support the change of energy.

The changing in the cells will be too much for those who have not prepared and worked on this process. They will not survive the pressure against the physical body. Those who have been attempting to prepare will have cells that are crystalline. You *need* to have your energy raised and your DNA reconnected from four to twelve at least. Because if not, your body will not be able to withstand the pressure.

WHO ARE CHADD & VIE?

CHADD is a sound frequency gifted expert and a living miracle from God. Thirty-two years of psychiatric-prescribed drugs ingested against his will, eight weeks in a coma due to depression from the drugs, and recovering from blindness, anemia, incompetence, anorexia—also due to these drugs/medicine. Though he kept a few "friends" around, it took his Aquarius coworker to nourish him back to perfect health and to reinsert him into the system. He was not reintroduced to life, left in solitude in his wheelchair until he met her, but now many want a piece of him and of his power! And others wants him kept into a foggy-state drugs!

VIE is French royalty, an American gifted energy healer, a light and sound therapist. She works directly through the source guidance a new vibratory energy, with the cosmic doctors and with Nikola Tesla. VIE is the founder of the Biostimulation Institute of Light and Sound, LLC.

CHADD and VIE are here to share their powerful gifts with you and to prepare you for the necessary steps for the ascension and beyond. It is not religious, neither a cult, and there is no teaching. It is knowledge. They both channel the Holy Spirit.

The purpose of the Biostimulation Institute of Light and Sound is the following:

- awakening new frequencies within one's being
- for humanity to embrace the light and sound of creation and to expand consciousness
- To defragment old programming and to replace it with the light and sound frequencies of the new Divine plan for the

ascension. Space will then be created to incorporate new harmonies in the body of the human, and through this, healing on all planes will occur.
- because the language of light is cosmic light intelligence, carried in color streams of consciousness a place where everything is possible
- To heal at the level of cause and symptoms and fully unlock your healing, incorrect vibration must be not only retuned but the energy also has to be raised and you must be reconnected to your angel.

We will open at least seven institutes around the globe and at strategic places as soon as we will have the necessary funds to do so. Only one dollar from each of you can make the difference.

Since 2003, VIE have presented the light and sound therapy at numerous and various places, like in Louise Hayes Convention's I Can Do It! (Orlando, Tampa, Vegas), also at the Optometrist Convention at Saint Pete, at the ND Convention in Vegas, and the Acupuncture Convention in Florida, and since 2009, CHADD and VIE together, several times, at the Body, Mind, Spirit Expo in Tampa and in Orlando.

Our young living website: www.youngliving.org/helene398498

Stem Cell Supplements

We are also distributors of RBC-LIFE as they have the only clinically proven stem cell supplement called Stem-Kine™.

Stem cell benefits made headlines of *Newsweek, Times, National Geographic,* and *Reader's Digest* magazines.

Stem cells are undifferentiated cells, produced in your bone marrow and adipose tissue, which have not yet developed into a specific cell type. They are released to circulate in the bloodstream. Normally when areas of the body are injured, the damaged tissues release enzymes that attract stem cells. The stem cells infiltrate into the injured tissues and develop into healthy new cells of that particular tissue, liver, heart, brain, bone, or other tissues. This action by stem cells is the body's natural repair and renewal system.

The development of Stem-Kine—A stem cell research scientist wanted to supply a height level of nutrition to bone marrow for optimum production of stem cells. He developed a blend of natural source ingredients prepared by a fermentation process. Tests showed that the formula provides nutritional support to bone marrow, helping/enabling it to produce a greater number of new adult stem cells.

The activity is similar to plant life, when you fertilize your garden with higher quality of nutrients from bone marrow to support natural stem cell development.

QUANTUM ENERGY HEALING STORY (ORLANDO, FLORIDA)

The moment I lay down a magnetic field gently cradled my body. The connection was made.

To set the scene nothing in the weeks prior to our session had I heard of VIE or "what she does". Our session thus came about only because of circumstances and the intuition "it felt right"... and drastic measures were needed to address all unpleasant unexpected suddenly surfacing in my family's legacy. The hours leading up to our session even had a resurgence of upsetting facts that triggered feelings of newfound anger and frustration in me.

I had no expectations, nor reservations about "what might or not take place" in session with VIE. I simply had full confidence that on bigger scale, it was something needed to release positive power and generate a shift back to wellbeing for me and the greater good of most.

To understand my descriptions below, please know I am a person who generally associates an image to all physical perceptions, someone who turns any verbal exchange into a comic strip book mental experience with my own constant pop up bubbles...

If I summarize my session with VIE, it was me being the exclusive front row spectator of my own beautiful "feel and light" performance. Please take note I deliberately use the word "performance" with meaning of "one's own ability" -- and not that of "one own acting".

By stating this comment above perhaps I have now voiced what has been puzzling me in my own family trials and tribulations of past three years.

I perceive VIE as an investigative journalist with intuitive hunch to feel or asks this and that so can ethically do "whatever it takes" for accurate facts to surface and be known. Whether course of action is taken from thereon by reader to value or not the reading of the article, will be entirely responsibility of said reader, not in any way the responsibility of the investigative reporter who never can impose or force the reader to anything.

I perceived our session as me being the choreographer of a spectacular ballet filled with graceful motions, uplifting lighting and flowing back drops and artists the analogy to my sought after harmony between colourful mental association and enhanced body awareness.

The 1st stage of our session was on physical awareness. I became aware of my left shoulder twinging, until realized all my fingers were magnetically drawn to the mattress. For the longest time my crooked left pinky demanded to have lots of attention, followed by other articulations, themselves heroes of past injuries/surgeries now claiming some TLC.

My mind took note how my left bodily parts positioned themselves very asymmetrically from their twin right side counterpart. Both my ankles were seemingly held down in a comforting way by unseen hands holding them from above firmly pressed grounded on bed.

My back soon enough drew attention to itself. If I recall correctly this was in conjunction with some needed emotional release for I was acutely aware of physical thoracic feeling that I was resting on a blunt spike poking upwards through the mattress, whilst the front of my rib cage projected forward and upwards as that of the prow sculpture of vintage buckaneer boats drawing all forward in motion.

VIE inquired about my hands. I noticed both had now turned themselves to face upwards. Right hand positioned itself as if cupping the underside of a rounded wine glass when my left one gave me the feeling of holding a large flat platter.

I remember a fleeting moment my neck transforming into a very heavy dark cannon ball plus the on and off awareness of "something" with my throat that also had to be released.

2nd stage was that of visual display stunningly dominated by the most radiant indigo blues with occasional purple hues. All patterns generally emerged indigo, then shifted swiftly to vibrant sunflower golden yellow. For undetermined time, I was mesmerized by this rhythmically flow and enlarging of truly exquisite artwork displays. The images went from flower buds opening up into oversized peonies likes shapes, to alternating between indigo blues and sunflower yellows full bouquets, to spectacular dark indigo manta rays powerfully ondulating across a black ocean under a fiery golden sky. There were a briefer vertical interchange of flowing screens as if curtains of coloured indigo to golden yellow rain.

The next powerful and very distinctive scenes were of peaceful atomic bomb like explosions of clouds, huge formations going from indigo to dark purple then fading to very light and "fluffy feeling" lavender tones before another the birth of another indigo explosion...

The 3rd stage and perhaps final part of our session, was VIE guiding me up 3 steps.

My instant vision was of a glowing cartoon style black back ground with a single sunflower yellow rectangle slightly off centred to the left. Suddenly one section took form and light up into a glowing 3D indigo step. This pattern was done one step at a time so all my focus was on that neon glow indigo blue that guided my footing. As if on a pressure motion, moment I was stepping off previous step the one immediately popped up glowing 3D indigo as previous one receded back into flat yellow rectangle. This is how made my way up into a bright dark oblivion where never saw anything else aside from one black bench upon which I sat waiting

9.1.1. Complete Guide to Natural Healing

to see what would appear in front of me. I had no expectations but did look intently but nothing/no one appeared. I just enjoyed basking in the most extraordinary intense full surrounds of luminous indigo blues vapors with feeling of elation.

I cannot recall accurately when exactly but another impacting moment was when in one of my indigo blisses, a round facetted diamond shape light appeared through the bleu veils much reminiscent of a luminous full moon shining through thin cloud coverage.

(International Client from Europe Gaby K.)

Other Books by VIE Loriot de Rouvray

Each volume of the books VIE wrote takes you on a journey for your growth, and your well-being. It is opening up your consciousness and expanding your mind to prepare your spirituality for the solar cycle 25 predicted. It will guide you back to the path of Oneness. Beware of the false prophets, Gurus and cults. Gold, silver, copper or lead will not help you ascend.

Destiny of the doG; Beware of the Almighty – Volume 1
Time is Ticking; The Fifth Amendment – Volume 2
Karma through the Window of Time – Volume 3
New Century, New Era, New Experiences – Volume 4
Intonex. The secret Harmony of Life.– Volume 5
The Genome of The Ancient Creators. – Volume 6
The Great Re-Call "The Radiant Light of the God Duo"- Volume 7
The Phoenix with the Crystal Plumage – Volume 8

Website: Instituteoflightandsound.com
https://facebook.com/VieLoriot
Video: Journey to the Fifth Dimension:
(https://www.youtube.com/watch?v=g4GSSZbXwzw)

VIE (*V*ibrational *I*ntuitive *E*nergy)
    Quantum Directed Light Energy –
    Body Frequency oscillation –
    Spiritual Counseling.

www.ingramcontent.com/pod-product-compliance
Lightning Source LLC
Chambersburg PA
CBHW021427070526
44577CB00001B/96